Reference Guides to Rhetoric and Composition
Series Editor, Charles Bazerman

REFERENCE GUIDES TO RHETORIC AND COMPOSITION
Series Editor, Charles Bazerman

The Series provides compact, comprehensive and convenient surveys of what has been learned through research and practice as composition has emerged as an academic discipline over the last half century. Each volume is devoted to a single topic that has been of interest in rhetoric and composition in recent years, to synthesize and make available the sum and parts of what has been learned on that topic. These reference guides are designed to help deepen classroom practice by making available the collective wisdom of the field and will provide the basis for new research. The Series is intended to be of use to teachers at all levels of education, researchers and scholars of writing, graduate students learning about the field, and all who have interest in or responsibility for writing programs and the teaching of writing.

Parlor Press and The WAC Clearinghouse are collaborating so that these books will be widely available through low-cost print editions and free digital distribution. The publishers and the Series editor are teachers and researchers of writing, committed to the principle that knowledge should freely circulate. We see the opportunities that new technologies have for further democratizing knowledge. And we see that to share the power of writing is to share the means for all to articulate their needs, interest, and learning into the great experiment of literacy.

EXISTING BOOKS IN THE SERIES
Invention in Rhetoric and Composition (2004, Lauer)
Reference Guide to Writing across the Curriculum (2005, Bazerman, Little, Bethel, Chavkin, Fouquette, and Garufis)
Revision: History, Theory, and Practice (2006, Horning and Becker)

Writing Program Administration

Susan H. McLeod

Parlor Press
West Lafayette, Indiana
www.parlorpress.com

The WAC Clearinghouse
http://wac.colostate.edu/

Parlor Press LLC, West Lafayette, Indiana 47906

© 2007 by Parlor Press and The WAC Clearinghouse
All rights reserved.
Printed in the United States of America

SAN: 254-8879

Library of Congress Cataloging-in-Publication Data

Writing program administration / [edited by] Susan H. McLeod.
    p. cm. -- (Reference guides to rhetoric and composition)
  Includes bibliographical references and index.
  ISBN 978-1-60235-007-6 (pbk. : alk. paper) -- ISBN 978-1-60235-008-3 (alk. paper) -- ISBN 978-1-60235-009-0 (adobe ebook)
  1. English language--Rhetoric--Study and teaching--United States. 2. Report writing--Study and teaching (Higher)--United States. 3. Writing centers--Administration. I. McLeod, Susan H.
  PE1405.U6W757 2007
  808'.0420711--dc22
                            2007009454

Series logo designed by Karl Stolley.
This book is printed on acid-free paper.

Parlor Press, LLC is an independent publisher of scholarly and trade titles in print and multimedia formats. This book is available in paperback, cloth, and Adobe eBook formats from Parlor Press on the World Wide Web at http://www.parlorpress.com. For submission information or to find out about Parlor Press publications, write to Parlor Press, 816 Robinson St., West Lafayette, Indiana, 47906, or e-mail editor@parlorpress.com.

The WAC Clearinghouse supports teachers of writing across the disciplines. Hosted by Colorado State University's Composition Program, it brings together four journals, three book series, and resources for teachers who use writing in their courses. This book will also be available free on the Internet at The WAC Clearinghouse (http://wac.colostate.edu/).

Contents

Preface	*vii*
Charles Bazerman	
Acknowledgments	*ix*
1 Introduction and Overview	*3*
Issues in Writing Program Administration	4
Organization and Scope of the Text	5
2 Distinctions and Definitions	*7*
The WPA in the Institution	7
The WPA as Unappreciated Wife	11
The WPA as Scholar	14
The WPA as Politician, Rhetor,	
Change Agent, Manager	17
The WPA as Leader 20	
3 A History of Writing Program Administration	*23*
The Beginnings	23
English Departments and Composition	24
The History of Rhetoric and the	
New Emphasis on English	27
Development of a Composition Underclass	31
The Pedagogy and Curricula of	
Early Composition Courses	32
The Tenacity of Current-Traditional Rhetoric	38
The Pre-Professional Period: Writing Program	
Administration up to World War II	45
The Period of Professionalization: Post World War II	58
The First Professional Organization	
for WPAs: CCCC	63
The Birth of the Council of	
Writing Program Administrators	67

The Development of *WPA: The Journal of Writing Program Administration*	76
Writing Program Administration in the Twenty-First Century	78

4 Current Issues and Practical Guidelines — 80

Curriculum	81
First-Year Composition	81
Basic Writing	85
ESL and Generation 1.5 Students	87
Articulation	88
Beyond First-Year Composition	88
Pedagogy	89
Assessment and Accountability	92
Overviews	92
Placement	94
Proficiency	95
Program Assessment	96
Staffing, Staff Development, and Evaluation	98
Administrative and Professional Issues	100

5 Glossary — 105

6 Practical Resources for Writing Program Administrators: A Selected Bibliography — 114
Anne Whitney

General Resource Guides/Overviews	114
Curriculum and Pedagogy	117
Assessment and Accountability	120
Staffing and Staff Development	124
Administrative and Professional Issues	128

Notes	132
Works Cited	136
Index	153

Preface

The teaching of writing in higher education almost always occurs within a writing program (or similar unit such as a department largely devoted to the teaching of writing) under the supervision and coordination of an administrator, often called a Writing Program Administrator (WPA). Furthermore, the field of teaching of writing has socially, economically, and historically been organized around writing programs. Finally, most people embarking on a career in the teaching of writing will at some point be engaged in administering a writing program. Surprisingly then, this volume offers the first overall history we have had of writing programs and their administration as a central organizing theme of the field. Understandably the field of teaching of writing has focused on the units of analysis all have had much experience of: being a writer, being a learner of writing, supporting learning of writing, and running a classroom devoted to the teaching and leaning of writing. Yet, just the next level up in the economic and institutional realities of administration, we gain a remarkable perspective on what the field of college composition is and how it has become that way. This is a story of interest to every teacher of college writing, whether or not they will be an administrator or are engaged in program policy issues.

On a more practical level, there has been a growing body of publications reporting the experiences of WPAs, providing practical advice, and surveying the nature and conditions of programs nationally. This fourth volume of the reference guides to rhetoric and composition provides an excellent introduction to this useful literature, so that anyone embarking on Writing Program Administration can explore the state of the art—and perhaps even more importantly connect up with the personal and publication networks WPA's have developed for mutual support. Nonetheless, despite there now being some collected wisdom based on the hard won experience of many dedicated and thoughtful people, we still have much to learn about this important role and the decisions facing administration. I hope this overview of our current state of knowledge will inspire a new generation of research and evidence to provide guidance and support for the writing programs of the future.

—*Charles Bazerman*

Acknowledgments

I have tried to write the book I wish I'd had when I first started as a WPA. My debts are many. I would like to thank Chuck Bazerman for inviting me to take on this project; David Russell, who reviewed the chapter on the history of writing program administration and gave me excellent feedback; Shirley Rose, who read the entire manuscript and also gave me good advice; UCSB librarian Sherri Barnes, who tirelessly tracked down elusive sources; the history graduate students in my Writing for Publication seminar, who helped me understand how difficult it is to write history; my colleagues on the WPA listserv, who gave me useful feedback on the glossary; Rebecca Mitchell, who copyedited an early version of the manuscript; Amy Ferdinandt Stolley, who created the index; David Blakesley, whose patience and good humor are unsurpassed among editors; and as always, my husband Doug, who supported and put up with me throughout. I am also grateful to two WPA mentors: Joyce Steward, who was my TA supervisor many years ago at the University of Wisconsin and who modeled the behavior of respect towards students and novice teachers that I have strived to emulate as a WPA, and Maxine Hairston, who led a WPA workshop that I had the great good fortune to attend in 1984 and who served as a role model for me in more ways than she knew.

Writing Program Administration

1 Introduction and Overview

Although the work involved in writing program administration has existed for some time (as documented in Chapter 3), it was not until the formation of the Council of Writing Program Administrators in the late 1970s that the work was dignified with a title that aligned it with other administrative positions in the university. Before that time, the job was usually a service task assigned to some faculty member (often to supervise TAs), and there was usually one per campus, in the English Department. That situation has changed radically in the last twenty years; not only has the title of Writing Program Administrator (WPA) caught on as a general descriptor for the intellectual as well as bureaucratic work involved in such positions, but also the number of different kinds of writing programs has grown. If you called some of the larger institutions of higher education in this country and asked to speak to the writing program administrator, you would be asked, "Which one?" At Purdue University, for example, you would find a Director and an Assistant Director of the Writing Lab, a Director and two Assistant Directors of Composition, a Director and an Assistant Director of the Professional Writing Program, and a Director of the ESL Writing Program. At Washington State University, there is a Director of Composition, a Director of Campus Writing Programs, a Director of Writing Assessment, and a Director and Assistant Director of the Writing Center. Other institutions have Directors of Basic Writing, Directors of Writing Across the Curriculum or Writing in the Disciplines, Composition Coordinators, Directors of Writing-Intensive Freshman Seminars, Directors of Business Writing, Coordinators of Upper-Division Writing, and in growing numbers, Chairs of Departments of Writing or of Writing Studies. All these are writing program administrators. This volume will focus on writing program administration within or among academic departments (usually English departments), with a focus on the administration of first-year writing programs, since that is still the most common kind of WPA work; it should be noted, though, that much of the present discussion also relates to writing program administration of other stripes.

Issues in Writing Program Administration

The issues in writing program administration, like those of any university administrative position, are numerous and varied. The administrator is called upon to respond to regular directives and deadlines (for budget proposals, five-year plans, personnel evaluations); because the job is driven by these and by various crises that arise (like budget cuts, grade complaints, seriously ill faculty), one must guard against being reactive rather than proactive as a WPA. Knowing what the basic issues are and making plans each year, perhaps each term, to allocate time and energy to the most important issues, can help a WPA plan administrative time wisely. The matrix below is one way to think about how to plan time and energy.

Administrative Issues	
Urgent and important	Urgent but not important
Not urgent but important	Not urgent and not important

We tend, because of the nature of administrative jobs, to deal with the top half of this matrix—always dealing with what is urgent. Experienced administrators deal with the left half—blocking out time for what is most important for the job and delegating or ignoring the rest.

The main issues a WPA deals with are curriculum and pedagogy, assessment and accountability, staffing and staff development, and professional and personal issues of various stripes, including tenure and promotion. Further, whether or not the WPA handles his or her own budget, knowledge of how budgets work in his or her own institution is essential. Graduate programs in rhetoric and composition, recognizing that many of their students will be hired immediately into WPA positions, have begun offering seminars in writing program administration. However, administration, like teaching, is experiential and therefore best learned in an apprenticeship, working with and observing someone who is experienced, taking on some of the tasks gradually and with supervision. Recognizing this fact, many institutions now hire new faculty as assistant directors of composition, a position from which a new faculty member can grow into the job of a WPA.

ORGANIZATION AND SCOPE OF THE TEXT

Because it is a reference guide, the book provides a summary of the literature in the field; the organization of the book follows the usual format for this series, *Reference Guides to Rhetoric and Composition*. Chapter 2 deals with distinctions and definitions of the term "writing program administration." Defining this term is more difficult than might first appear; although there are many similarities among positions that involve writing program administration, there are also significant differences. Chapter 3 outlines the history of writing program administration in the U.S., with some background on both the development of first-year composition (a uniquely American course) and on the tenacious history of current-traditional rhetoric, an issue that WPAs must still deal with in many programs. Chapter 4 focuses on current views of the most important issues in Writing Program Administration as they appear in the literature and practical guidelines as to how to deal with them. Those new to the concept of writing program administration might want to read this chapter before reading the history chapter. Chapter 5 is a glossary of useful terms and abbreviations. The final chapter is an annotated bibliography of useful resources for writing program administrators.

I have tried to present the literature in the field as the authors themselves would have the work presented, as objectively as I can. However, I should acknowledge here my own personal biases in terms of administrative theory and practice. My work as a WPA has been informed by two major influences: my training and experience as an agent of change in the U.S. Peace Corps in the 1960s, and my experience in the Bryn Mawr Summer Seminar for Women in Higher Education Administration in the 1980s. It was at Bryn Mawr that I first encountered Rosabeth Moss Kanter's *The Change Masters,* a study of successful organizational change in business. Kanter's research resonated with my own experiences in both the Peace Corps and as a WPA. It helped me articulate my own vision of writing program administration as an activity that aims at bringing about institutional change in the way writing is viewed and taught in higher education—away from a view of writing courses as remediation and an accompanying current/traditional pedagogical approach, towards an acknowledgment of writing as intertwined with learning and critical thinking and a pedagogy that treated students with the respect due to neophytes learning ways of doing things in a new culture, that of academe.

2 Distinctions and Definitions

THE WPA IN THE INSTITUTION

Defining writing program administration should be easy, since it is that which writing program administrators (WPAs) do: define that administrative role in both institutional and intellectual terms and you have defined the work. But because writing programs are site-specific, they differ widely from one another, meaning that the work also differs widely from campus to campus. Consider these two job ads, modeled on ones that appeared recently:

1. Assistant Professor and Director of First-Year Writing: As Director of the first-year writing program, mentor and supervise adjunct composition faculty; supervise and train Writing Center tutors; offer composition/writing theory workshops for faculty; sponsor writing across the curriculum initiatives and other composition-related ventures. Teaching may include professional writing and history of the English language as well as writing courses. St. Clarence University is an independent Catholic institution in the liberal arts tradition, with 1,200 students and 70 faculty.

2. Advanced Assistant or Associate Professor and Writing Program Administrator, the University of Euphoric State: The WPA will be responsible for supervising adjuncts, lecturers, and graduate teaching assistants who teach freshman and junior writing; preparing TAs to teach; directing the composition program as appropriate to the university's mission; and providing leadership in curriculum development within the writing program. The WPA must be an active researcher of writing and knowledgeable in at least two of the following areas: writing in the disciplines, writing program administration, assessment, educational technol-

ogy and writing, technical writing, service learning, first-year experience. UES is a doctoral/research institution; the English Department has 30 full-time faculty and offers a BA, MA, and PhD in English as well as a graduate certificate in the teaching of writing.

These two ads illustrate a major feature of writing program administration: the fact that context is all. As Thomas Amorose notes in "WPA Work at the Small College or University," the WPA at an institution of under 5,000 students might be part of a department of seven departmental faculty (in English, or perhaps in Humanities or Communication Arts), where all faculty teach writing and where the major part of the administrative side of the job is working with these faculty in collegial ways, helping design curricula for writing courses, working with the Chair on scheduling, and heading up any testing efforts for placement or writing competency. He or she would teach a number of different undergraduate courses, since the department is small and the curricular needs legion. As David Schwalm notes in "The Writing Program (Administrator) in Context: Where Am I, and Can I Still Behave Like a Faculty Member?," such a job is a *task* rather than a *position;* it includes no particular standing in the administrative hierarchy and is often ill defined and open-ended. It is instead quasi-administrative, characterized by a lot of responsibility but no authority and no budget (9). The work of such a WPA is often counted in a performance review under the heading of "service," even though it is much more complex than the committee work that falls under that rubric for other faculty. At a large research institution like the one advertising the second position, a WPA might be part of a department of 30 or more tenure-track faculty members, along with 20 or 30 adjuncts and as many TAs. Besides working out the curricula for the various writing courses, he or she would be in charge of TA training, of finding ways to integrate the adjuncts into the program without treating them like superannuated TAs, and of teaching graduate courses (often pedagogy courses for the TAs but sometimes also the methods courses for secondary education, courses in rhetoric, creative writing, technical writing, and literature). This person would also handle grade complaints; plagiarism issues; staffing, hiring, evaluating, and sometimes firing TAs and adjuncts; working with the administration and other institutions on articulation agreements; and planning or helping to plan the program's budget. This sort of WPA is in effect the head of a department within a department, and usually receives some released time from teaching in recognition of that fact. There is usually a place in the departmental organizational chart for this person (along with the associate chair and perhaps other positions); the person therefore has positional authority and a set of duties and expectations outlined in the bylaws. So although there are common administrative tasks and assignments among all WPA positions, the definition of a writing program administrator is very much site-specific, dependent on local history (e.g., how the program has been shaped by local exigencies such as state mandates for assessment) and the size and complexity of the institution. As Jeanne Gunner notes in "Decentering the WPA," the position is often amorphous; definition is problematic and therefore a crucial problem (8). Without a clear definition of the work, WPAs sometimes find themselves in positions that others define for them in unrealistic ways.

Further, WPA work differs from other university administrative jobs in two important ways. First, WPAs—unlike most other administrators—are doing work (involving curriculum, assessment, placement, and staff development/TA training) that is directly linked to and informed by a growing body of research in their own scholarly field. When a dean asks whether or not students can't just be placed in writing classes based on their SAT verbal scores, the WPA can, and should, respond with research on placement methods that demonstrates better ways of determining which students should be placed in which courses, including directed self-placement. When a department chair wants to increase the cap on writing class size, the WPA can produce the NCTE guidelines on class size, marshal the evidence on research on class size in higher education, and present the data on workload issues for teachers of composition (see Chapter 4). Unlike the situation even twenty years ago, there is now a solid research base for many of the administrative decisions with which the WPA is faced. Second, because the first-year writing course is usually the only course that all students in the institution are required to take, the WPA is in a unique institutional position, answerable not only to the department chair but also in effect to the entire university. Because faculty often have a reductive ("no surface errors") and sometimes uniquely personal ("writes like me") notion of what good student writing looks like, this can put the WPA in the position of being held accountable for the general state of student writing across campus.

The definition of the term "writing program" also differs from institution to institution. As Schwalm notes, "a collection of courses taught by various faculty according to their own lights and probably not desiring much direction" cannot be considered a program. He goes on to say:

> A writing *program* minimally consists of one or more courses (usually first-year courses) with multiple sections of each, governed by a common set of objectives. They might also have a common course syllabus, some consistency in teaching methods, and common assessment and placement procedures. There are lots of add-ons and variations. As WPA, your portfolio might include additional courses, such as advanced composition, technical communication, or business writing. The responsibilities sometimes include basic writing, a writing center, and placement and assessment processes. You may be responsible for writing across the curriculum programs (WACs) as well [. . .]. There is no agreed-upon concept of "writing program." There is no reason why there must be agreement, and again, no particular model is necessarily better than another [. . .]. (11)

Experienced WPA's have written about understanding the WPA's role within the institution. Schwalm divides the organization of almost all universities into three major administrative units: academic affairs, student affairs, and administrative affairs. Within academic affairs, most important to understand is the academic "chain of command" (a structure with some similarities to the management structures of late nineteenth-century corporations, since it developed in parallel with those structures). The chair of a department is the front-line manager, reporting to a dean (a middle manager); the academic dean reports to a central administrator, often a provost or academic vice president, whose job is to be the chief academic officer (CAO). This person is usually the most dominant figure on the academic side of the house, since he or she usually controls the flow of the budget (12–14). These positions are known as line positions; one usually rises through the faculty ranks to ever-higher levels of responsibility. Non-line administrative positions often include deans or vice provosts for graduate/

undergraduate studies and vice presidents/provosts for research, diversity, finances, student affairs, extended services, summer sessions, etc. Although many WPA positions differ from all these in that they are usually located within departmental structures, there are some similarities, in that the WPA is responsible for what is usually viewed as a program that serves the entire campus. A clear understanding of the administrative hierarchy is crucial for making that program work, but an understanding of who does what in the other parts of the university is also key. Schwalm notes that there is a simple rule to follow regardless of where the WPAs position lies in this hierarchy: "Make friends among the master sergeants. One friendly associate registrar is worth more than a roomful of deans when it comes to getting things done" (14).

The WPA as Unappreciated Wife

Although WPAs are like other university administrators in some ways, they may be different from most of their administrative colleagues in terms of seniority. A line administrator in higher education is nearly always a tenured member of the faculty, usually a full professor, someone who has proven him/herself first as a member of the faculty. Although they do not always rise through the faculty ranks as do line administrators, most non-line administrators are likewise senior members of the community, people who have wide experience with university matters: because these managerial positions are leadership positions, seniority and experience are important for success. The WPA, however, may be taking on an administrative position as an untenured assistant professor (see the two job ads, above), a situation which has its dangers. Unless the letter of hire specifies exactly how WPA work counts as intellectual and scholarly work (as spelled out by the Council of Writing Program Administrators), tenure committees may count the work only as "service" and deny tenure as a result. The new WPA must be very mindful of this possibility.

The situation is complicated by the genderized nature of composition as a field. As we shall see in the next chapter, after a brief period at Harvard when highly respected members of academe were in charge, the teaching of composition became relegated to teaching assistants and contingent faculty. Many of the latter were women, in part because of the fact that academe was (up until the affirmative action regulations of the 1970s) a decidedly male-dominated organization, and also because women who married and had families were not expected to work full-time, if they worked at all. Theresa Enos describes this gendering process in *Gender Roles and Faculty Lives in Rhetoric and Composition*. Summarizing the work of a number of scholars, she lists the factors that have helped to define composition as "women's work": it has a disproportionate number of women workers, it is service-oriented, and it pays less than "men's work"[1] and is therefore devalued (4). Sue Ellen Holbrook (in "Women's Work: The Feminizing of Composition") demonstrates how the hierarchical nature of English studies made it easier for women to find jobs in the lower tier because of the belief of the male literature faculty that composition was "drudge work" and that teaching composition was just that (207). The director's role, then, became that of "wife." Charles Schuster, in an essay on the politics of promotion within English departments, enlarges on this definition: WPAs are "dutiful wives who do much of the dirty work: teaching writing, reading myriad student essays, training TAs and lecturers, administering testing programs. That is the primary function of the composition wives; to maintain the house and raise the children, in this case the thousands of undergraduates who enroll in composition classes" (88). Lynn Bloom caricatured this definition of writing program administration in an essay entitled "I Want a Writing Director," a piece modeled on Judy Syfer's "I Want a Wife" (a famous feminist skewering of gender roles that appeared in the preview edition of *Ms.* magazine[2] in December, 1971).

> I want a Writing Director who will keep the writing program out of my hair. I want a Writing Director who will hire a cadre of part-time comp teachers to teach all the freshpersons. I want the Writing Director to be a woman and to hire primarily women because women are more nurturing, they are usually available on the campus where their husbands or other Significant Others teach, and besides, they will work for a lot lower salary than men and can get along without benefits. The money my school saves by hiring these part-timers can be applied toward my full-time salary [. . .] [I]f by chance she does not meet our department's rigorous criteria for tenure—after all, we have our standards to maintain—I want the

> liberty to replace the present Writing Director with another one. (176, 177)

Noting the genderized nature of the field, feminist scholars in composition have taken up the issue of power as part of the role of the WPA. Rebecca Moore Howard critiques the portrait of the agonistic, individualistic WPA outlined by Edward White (in "Use It or Lose It"), advocating instead an approach that refuses a "militaristic" spirit in favor of "collective methods for effecting change . . . that will transgress the discourse of hierarchical competition" (40), and Marcia Dickson proposes a feminist definition of writing program administration that seeks collaboration and joint problem-solving rather than power brokering. Hildy Miller, in "Postmasculinist Directions in Writing Program Administration," summarizes the discussions of feminist administration, asking what she terms basic questions: "First of all, what does 'feminist directing' look like in actual practice? Secondly, in what ways does a delivery system informed by feminist ideology clash with the masculinist administrative structures in which it is embedded? And, finally, how can two such seemingly incompatible systems be made to mesh into a 'postmasculinist' approach?" (50). With a caveat that the terms she is using are risky (in that they smack of essentialism), she defines feminist administration as cooperative, participatory, egalitarian, integrating the cognitive and the affective, the personal and the professional. Miller points out that, although this approach is effective in some instances (reaching out to an angry parent to express shared concern about a student who is failing), feminist approaches are likely to be misinterpreted as weakness from a masculinist point of view. Miller argues for a definition of writing program administration as both feminist and masculinist.

> As a matter of practicality, the two must merge. After all, masculinist assumptions about power, leadership, and administration permeate the academy, affecting feminist approaches at every turn. Merging the two requires a WPA to take a bi-epistemological stance. As a marginalized group, women have historically learned to function in two worlds. Compositionists who apply feminist principles in the classroom do the same. Thus it is not surprising that WPAs would also need to employ these strategies [. . .]. The postmas-

> culinist, then, is not just a matter of replacing masculinist with feminist, but rather of somehow doing both or creating a space for one to exist within the other. (58)

The WPA as Scholar

In the 1980s there was an abundance of anecdotal evidence that young WPAs were being denied tenure as a result of their departments not understanding or caring about the nature of their administrative work (see Chapter 4). In part to combat the definition of WPA as unappreciated and therefore disposable wife, the Council of Writing Program Administrators developed a set of guidelines for the work entitled "The Portland Resolution: Guidelines for Writing Program Administrator Positions."[3] The first of these guidelines, developing clear job descriptions, is then presented in some detail, outlining the preparation a WPA should have in terms of knowledge and experience and the responsibilities of the job (including the scholarship of administration; faculty development and other teaching; writing program development; writing assessment; writing program assessment; and accountability, registration and scheduling, office management, counseling and advising, and articulation). The document was meant to be helpful to departments advertising for WPA positions and to WPAs searching for ways to define what they did in ways that their colleagues could understand.

The Executive Committee of Council of Writing Program Administrators also developed a related document to expand on the second guideline mentioned, that of establishing clear criteria for assessing the work of a WPA, determining how administrative work should be evaluated for tenure and promotion. A draft of this second document appeared in the Fall/Winter 1996 volume of *WPA: Writing Program Administration,* appearing in final form in 1998 as a position statement, "Evaluating the Intellectual Work of Writing Program Administration."[4] The Preamble to the position statement is worth quoting at length.

> It is clear within departments of English that research and teaching are generally regarded as intellectual, professional activities worthy of tenure and

promotion. But administration—including leadership of first-year writing courses, WAC programs, writing centers, and the many other manifestations of writing administration—has for the most part been treated as a management activity that does not produce new knowledge and that neither requires nor demonstrates scholarly expertise and disciplinary knowledge. While there are certainly arguments to be made for academic administration, in general, as intellectual work, that is not our aim here. Instead, our concern is to present a framework by which writing administration can be seen as scholarly work and therefore subject to the same kinds of evaluation as other forms of disciplinary production such as books, articles, and reviews. More significantly, by refiguring writing administration as scholarly and intellectual work, we argue that it is worthy of tenure and promotion when it advances and enacts disciplinary knowledge within the field of Rhetoric and Composition. (Council 85)

The Position Statement presents several case studies, and then, following Christine Hult's lead in her essay "The Scholarship of Administration," invokes Ernest Boyer's *Scholarship Reconsidered: Priorities of the Professoriate,* to define writing program administration in one of Boyer's categories: the Scholarship of Application. The authors note that Boyer does not argue that all service should be lumped into this category. "To be considered scholarship, scholarship activities must be tied directly to one's special field of knowledge and relate to, and flow directly out of, this professional activity. Such service is serious, demanding work, requiring the rigor—and the accountability—traditionally associated with research activities" (Boyer 22). To be considered scholarship, the Position Statement concludes, writing program administration must meet two tests. It first needs to advance knowledge—knowledge production, clarification, connection, reinterpretation, or application. Second, it should result in products or activities that others can evaluate; the statement quotes a list of qualities from an essay entitled *The Disciplines Speak* which "seem to characterize that work that most disciplines would consider 'scholarly' or 'professional'":

- the activity requires a high level of discipline-related expertise.
- the activity is [. . .] innovative.
- the activity can be replicated or elaborated.
- the work and its results can be documented.
- the work and its results can be peer-reviewed.
- the activity has significance or impact. (Diamond and Adam 14)

The Position Statement lists five categories of intellectual work that can be figured into a definition of writing program administration as the scholarship of application: program creation, curricular design, faculty development, program assessment, and program-related textual production (not just conference papers or articles in refereed journals but also innovative syllabi, funding proposals, statements of philosophy for the curriculum, resources for staff training, etc.), and offers guidelines for evaluating this work.

In an article that was intended as a supplement to this document ("The WPA as Pragmatist: Recasting 'Service' as 'Human Science'"), Donald Bushman offers another way of classifying the intellectual work of a WPA by viewing it through the lens of pragmatist philosophy, two principle elements of which are reflection and action (31).

Bushman summarizes pragmatist theories from John Dewey and George Herbert Mead, key figures in the educational reform movement of the early twentieth century, pointing out that Dewey scorned the traditional hierarchy view of "knowing" (purely mental activity) as superior to "doing." Bushman argues that the WPA as pragmatist is both a doer and a knower. Pointing to Louise Weatherbee Phelps's definition of composition as a human science, Bushman states: "when we see our jobs [. . .] through the lens of Phelps's characterization of composition instruction—as a complex, 'experimental' activity—we see composition and the job of a WPA as an intellectual undertaking that is concerned with action and reflection; we see it as praxis" (40). Two books edited by Shirley Rose and Irwin Weiser, *The Writing Program Administrator as Theorist* and *The Writing Program Administrator as Researcher*, have deepened the discussion of writing program administration as scholarship. *Theorist* is made up of essays that focus on theorizing various issues of programs and administration, including leadership theories, ethical issues, writing across the curriculum, collaborative research, and assessment. *Researcher* contains essays that focus on approaches to research that provide feedback loops into the writing program as well as ways of turning the administrative work into published scholarship. The essays discuss feminist methodology as it relates to WPA inquiry, historical research as applied to local programs (especially archival research), research using surveys and outcomes assessment, and assessment of teacher preparation programs.

THE WPA AS POLITICIAN, RHETOR, CHANGE AGENT, MANAGER

As Doug Hesse points out in "Politics and the WPA," WPAs are both politicians and rhetors. Kenneth Bruffee (in an interview quoted in Amy Heckathorn's dissertation) emphasizes these two roles, discussing the uniqueness of the WPA job as a subversive activity conducted by people able to make changes that are important because they themselves are not that visible.

> It's a low level job that has aspects to it that no other low level academic job has. It's not like a department chair, for example [. . .]. WPAs are right out there because they are talking to those chairs and trying to get them to do something they don't want to do [. . .], You are constantly working the system in a way that's really very exciting. It's hard to think of a comparable occupation. I suppose it must be a little bit like at some level being a legislator must be[. . .]. It's really politicking of a genuinely republican sense [. . .]. [A]s a WPA you function and get a lot of the same kinds of kicks you would get as a Provost—being able to deal at large with the whole university, not just the department—because what you are doing is understood by the university to be somehow relevant to practically every part of it. Much of the level is low enough—you're a submarine—you can do the same things you could only get to do if you were running the whole show. (158–60)

Susan McLeod also discusses the subversive nature of the WPA in "The Foreigner: WAC Directors as Agents of Change." Although the focus is specifically on WAC directors, the discussion is relevant to the role of all WPAs in representing their program to outside constituencies, especially administrators or faculty from other departments on campus who express concern about student writing. McLeod discusses various roles that WPAs are often cast in by virtue of the language used by administrators to describe their university-wide role (e.g., the conqueror, the diplomat, the missionary), proposing that WPAs should invent a new role for themselves, that of change agent, working to change curricula and pedagogy to line up with what we know about learning theory.

Like it or not, WPAs are also managers: they function within an administrative structure, most often an English department, reporting to a line administrator such as a chair or a department head. Although they are also faculty members and as such focus on the needs of students, they must as WPAs act in the interests of the program and the institution. This managerial role has been critiqued at some length by various members of the profession. James Sledd, in a scathing essay that began as an address to the 1990 Conference of Writing Program Administrators, defined writing program administrators as "boss compositionists," overseers of poorly paid contingent faculty and TAs, complicit in the English department indifference to the exploitation of these groups and in upholding the dominance of literary studies. He describes what he saw than as the prevalent solution to the fraught relationship between literature and composition:

> to keep composition in departments devoted primarily to literature, to placate the boss compositionists by admitting them to the worshipful company of privileged researchers, but still to assign the actual teaching of writing to the contingent workers and teaching assistants. With that solution the compositionists are apparently content, since it marks the literary establishment's acceptance of their claims to share the glory. (275)

Donna Strickland has examined the history of composition programs through the lens of management science, showing how many of the practices that administrators now must deal with (like a heavy reliance on part-time labor) are a result of nineteenth century "scientific" managerial theories and practices. The managerial role of WPA has also been defined and critiqued from a Marxist perspective by Marc Bousquet ("Composition as a Management Science"); he sees the WPA as a low-level administrator, a "non-commissioned officer" whose task is "to creatively theorize and enact procedures to the disadvantage of other workers" (498). Citing an essay by James Porter and his colleagues that calls for composition specialists to be managerial insiders working to bring about change in universities, he states that "education management and its rhetoric of the past thirty years . . . has created the institution we need to change" (494). He offers instead "a labor theory of agency and a rhetoric of solidarity" (494), ridding universities of WPAs and practicing "social-movement unionism" (517. Bousquet continued his critique in a co-edited volume entitled *Tenured Bosses and Disposable Teachers: Writing Instruction in the Managed University*.)

Faculty and TA unions have in fact begun to spring up across the country, but administrative roles show no signs of disappearing as a result. Unionization has, however, called into question the definition of all university administrators: are they labor (because they are also faculty) or are they management? In "Doin' the Managerial Exclusion: What WPAs Might Need to Know about Collective Bargaining," Rita Malenczyk reviews how courts and labor boards have defined university administration in general with this caveat: "If those of us who are union members (as well as those who are not) do not know where and why the law has historically placed people who do what we do, then we may be unpleasantly surprised when we find our jobs—and ourselves—defined by a discourse we had no idea we were part of" (23). Malenczyk reviews a key 1980 Supreme Court decision, *National Labor Relations Board v. Yeshiva University* (known in collective bargaining circles simply as *Yeshiva*). The issue at hand was whether or not Yeshiva faculty had the right to unionize; the NLRB had ruled they could, but the university's stance was that faculty were excluded under the National Labor Relations Act of 1935. That act, which governs private schools, distinguishes among employees, professional employees, and supervisors (managers): the first two can unionize, since they are presumed to act in their own interests, but the latter—who are presumed to act in the interest of the employer—cannot. Yeshiva University argued successfully that all faculty were managerial employees, since they have significant influence over university policy, thereby effectively barring all faculty at private institutions from unionizing. The Supreme Court's decision was 5–4, however, and Malenczyk points out that the dissenting minority objected to this definition, pointing out that education has become "big business," a process that has eroded the faculty's role in decision-making. In other court decisions the differing interpretations of managerial roles have persisted—for example, chairs of departments at Boston University were found not to be subject to the "managerial exclusion" in a 1978 case, a different conclusion than the one that had been reached in a 1976 case involving the University of Vermont. Malenczyk concludes: "Any time a faculty at a state college or university unionizes, the state labor board decides upon composition of the union, and makes its decisions in part by looking at the duties of the faculty on a particular campus. Such faculty might be writing program directors or writing center directors as well as department chairs, and they are subject to a variety of state and local laws which differ tremendously from one another as well as from (in some cases) the NLRA [National Labor Relations Act]" (29). In spite of the fact that the university may define all administrators (including WPAs) as managers, the legal definition of administrative positions can vary enormously, depending on state and local laws, in terms of whether they are labor or management.

THE WPA AS LEADER

Irene Ward discusses the role of WPA as leader as well as manager, emphasizing the leadership aspect as the process of establishing the vision of the program, while the managerial aspect involves implementing the vision. Ward points to recent theories in leadership that shift the emphasis on a single influential person to "productive interpersonal relationships that empower all to succeed. The new leaders are not merely charismatic; they don't enforce a personal vision to which others must adhere or leave. They are vehicles of empowerment and agency in those whom '*they serve*'" (63). Ward quotes the research on power in social situations, concluding that the sources of power for WPAs are "expert power"—the fact that they have the knowledge to get things done, and "referent power"—derived from what sort of persons they are, their *ethos,* as observed in how they treat others. Ward points out that these new definitions of leadership for the information age will resonate with WPAs, since they involve such buzzwords as respect, understanding, appreciation, and interconnectedness, and speak of leadership as teaching and learning (64).

Barbara L. Cambridge and Ben W. McClelland make a related argument in "From Icon to Partner: Repositioning the Writing Program Administrator." They refer to Helen Astin and Carol Leland's *Women of Influence, Women of Vision,* a book that posits two kinds of leaders, positional and nonpositional. A positional leader is one who provides leadership within an organization as a result of his or her position in the organizational structure, while a nonpositional leader is one who produces knowledge (for example, as a scholar). "The position of WPA demands that one be both a positional and nonpositional leader, existing in a wide network of administrators, scholars, teachers students, and other publics who expect excellence in both kinds of leadership" (Cambridge and McClelland 153). Because of the complexity of this sort of leadership (and also to ensure that WPAs do not wind up being the one person on a campus charged with everything having to do with student writing), Cambridge and McClelland make suggestions about how to spread the power and authority on a sort of Federalist model. One way to do this is, they suggest, to follow John Gardner's advice, and manage interconnectedness. Gardner lists five skills that are needed for such management:

1. agreement building, including skills in conflict resolution, mediation, compromise, and coalition building;

2. networking, building the linkages to get things done;

3. exercising nonjurisdictional power, relying not on position but on the power of ideas, the power that belongs to those who understand systems;

4. institution building, including building systems that institutionalize problem solving; and

5. flexibility, including the willingness to redefine one's role at any time. (119)

This brings us back to the issue raised at the beginning of this chapter: that in spite of the commonalities in terms of the intellectual work involved, writing program administrators' actual positions vary greatly, with the result that there is no single definition of "writing program administration" or "writing program administrator." In an online conversation about writing up job descriptions for WPAs, David Schwalm argued that the task of definition should be individual: "WPAs should define their jobs, set goals in each area (research, teaching, service, administration), and identify measures of success." Given the variety of exigencies and contexts within which writing program administrators work, the most workable definition of writing program administration is one written (and rewritten) for the job at hand.

3 A History of Writing Program Administration

The Beginnings

Writing program administration has from the beginning been tied to freshman (or first-year) composition, a peculiarly American institution: there was until very recently no comparable course in universities based on the European model.[1] To understand the history of writing program administration and to understand the politics still surrounding the position of WPA, one must go back to the beginnings of this unique course, since the institutional structures that gave birth to the course and the attitudes towards it are still very much with us today. And as Robert Connors reminds us, by

> studying the ways in which composition was formed both by choice and by necessity, we learn who we are, come to understand more clearly the power we hold and constraints upon us. Through a better understanding of how we as teachers and scholars came to exist, we can perhaps understand more clearly the complex forces that make up our special discipline and work more successfully within these forces. ("Historical Inquiry" 158)

The essays in James J. Murphy's *A Short History of Writing Instruction* demonstrate that although instruction in the composition of discourse has been a part of instruction in rhetoric in the West since 500 BCE, it was not until the nineteenth century that universities began to shift from a focus on oral to written production, and from a focus on reading, speaking, and translating the classical languages to a focus on English as the language of instruction and learning. Writing went from being a script for oral production to a skill thought necessary for professional life in an increasingly technological economy with a rising middle class. Although they deal with writing program administration only tangentially, several historians of the field have traced the events and influences that led to the creation of a separate course, usually within an English department. These histories, along with others that trace the development of faculty hiring patterns and of current-traditional rhetoric, help to explain the professional context in which many WPAs still operate. As Connors says, "We continue to inhabit a professional world directly shaped by our history" ("Historical Inquiry" 160).

In writing this brief history of writing program administration, I have been guided by the work of Robert Connors, as articulated in three of his articles: "Writing the History of Our Discipline," "Dreams and Play: Historical Method and Methodology," and "Historical Inquiry in Composition Studies." Although the purpose of this volume is to serve as a reference and therefore summarize existing research, there is as yet no comprehensive history of writing program administration to summarize. Therefore I have felt it necessary to add original material as necessary to fill in some of the gaps. In this, as in the choice of material to use as I mapped out the history, I have followed a fairly traditional historical model (as did Connors), relying on published sources. I recognize that the alternative model of historical research, based on the model of the *Annales* School in France, would also examine memoranda, journals, assignments, minutes of university committees, handouts, and student papers. Some general work has been done in this area (for example, Wozniack, Masters), but a more comprehensive history of writing program administration will depend on many more such studies that include administrative work as part or all of the focus. The discipline of history itself continues to grapple with the notion of history and objectivity, noting the postmodern fact that no history is entirely objective (Novick); I therefore present this narrative as a sketch, a first attempt for others to fill in or correct as needed.

English Departments and Composition

At their beginnings, American colleges (there were no universities) such as Harvard were private, sectarian,[2] undergraduate affairs of at most a few hundred students; their mission was to prepare an elite group of young men for the Protestant ministry, teaching, or public life. If one wanted a doctorate, one had to go to Europe, usually to a German university. There were no separate departments; faculty often taught multiple subjects within the classical curriculum. The administrative structure usually consisted of a board of trustees (made up of clergymen), a president, and the faculty; as Connors notes, "very few colleges were so large that all administration could not be carried out personally" ("Rhetoric in the Modern University: The Creation of an Underclass" 56), usually by the president. The administrative model was that of the family, with the president as the paterfamilias, in charge of almost every detail of college life. For example, John Witherspoon, a Presbyterian minister and President of Princeton University during the period of the American Revolution, served as president and principal orator of the college, and in addition "was the chairman of the Philosophy Department, of the History Department, and of what today we would call the English Department, and gave sermons in the college chapel every Sunday. In addition, he tutored students in French and Hebrew" (Herman 144).

All this changed after the Civil War. Responding to the growing influence of science and technology in the late nineteenth century, American universities changed radically in just one generation: they did away with the classical curriculum in favor of an elective system, developed disciplinary specialties and departments, and focused on developing students for an expanding number of professions. They also grew larger and more complex, requiring more oversight and therefore more administrators (between 1890 and 1910 enrollments almost doubled, and by 1920 had almost doubled again; see Connors, "Rhetoric in the Modern University" 80–81; Cremin 545; Veysey 4). To meet the demand for trained elementary and secondary school teachers, normal schools opened to provide teacher training. In 1839 there was a grand total of three students enrolled in one normal school; by 1875 there were 22,000 students in 82 different institutions (Harper 80). In part because of the ongoing influence of those in the abolitionist movement after the Civil War, colleges were founded for African Americans to open higher education to a group that had (by law in many states) been denied any education at all. Although there were some colleges for women before the Civil War, the number of these increased dramatically as the women's suffrage movement (which grew out of the abolitionist movement) pushed for women's rights. The Morrill Act of 1862 established public Land Grant Universities that emphasized applied arts such as engineering, agriculture, and home economics. These institutions were specifically aimed at those who had heretofore not been able to afford a college education, those the Act referred to as "the industrial classes." As Robert Connors notes in *Composition-Rhetoric: Backgrounds, Theory, and Pedagogy*, this brought a new population of students to American higher education. "From the province of a small group of elite students, college education became, during this time, much more available to the masses. The colleges suddenly found themselves with students who needed to be taught to write, who needed to be taught correctness in writing, who needed to know forms, and who could be run through the system in great numbers. Composition-rhetoric after the Civil War evolved to meet these needs" (9). The course we now know as freshman composition became an almost universal requirement very quickly, located by historical accident in new disciplinary units called English Departments.

William Riley Parker's classic "Where Do English Departments Come From?," an essay based on the talk he gave at a meeting of the Association of Departments of English (an organization for English Department chairs), helps in part to explain why the relationship between literature and composition has been and still remains uneasy. Parker uses a domestic metaphor to explain the formation of these disciplinary units in the late 1800s as a product of the marriage between oratory (eldest daughter of rhetoric) and philology (a field based on the German tradition of scientific inquiry, gradually superseded by linguistics). The marriage was unhappy and brief—oratory broke away to form departments of speech, and philology, morphing into linguistics, either struck out on its own as well or formed a happy alliance with anthropology. (The Speech Association of America was formed in 1914, the Linguistic Society of America in 1924.) English departments were left with a focus on literature, allying themselves with language departments in that regard and with them forming the Modern Language Association in 1883, to distinguish these languages from those studied in the classical curriculum.

How did it happen that composition became part of English? As Parker points out, there was no particular reason that the teaching of writing should have been entrusted to teachers of English language and literature; teaching language meant teaching it historically and comparatively, not teaching students how to write. But during the last quarter of the nineteenth century university enrollments doubled. "So long as there had been a narrow, prescribed curriculum and not too many students, departments of instruction had little or no administrative significance"; it was not until the 1890s that "departments became important administrative units, pigeonholes into which one dropped all the elements of a rapidly expanding curriculum" and college officials began to delegate to those units such tasks as deciding on issues of personnel and curriculum (348). Perhaps inevitably, departments became ambitious and competitive for resources; English began to eye unoccupied territory, including writing, for acquisition. In 1888 the "Committee of Ten" of the National Education Association recommended that literature and written composition be a unified high school course, and college entrance exams thereafter involved writing about literature. Composition became identified as part of something called English, a department which itself was, in Parker's words "the catchall for the work of teachers of extremely diverse interests and training, united theoretically but not actually by their common use of the mother tongue," part of a discipline that has never really defined itself (348). Speaking as the chair of an English department himself, Parker stated that "the history of our profession inspires in me very little respect for departments of English; their story is one of acquisitiveness, expediency, and incredible stupidity. I care a lot about liberal education, and I care a lot about the study of literature in English, but it seems to me that English departments have cared much less about liberal education and their own integrity than they have about their administrative power and prosperity" (350). Part of that prosperity involved and still involves teaching composition, the cash cow of most English departments. By gaining control of the teaching of writing, English departments gained control of the only universally required course, and therefore large enrollments, making it one of the biggest (and in some cases most powerful) departments in the university.

The History of Rhetoric and the New Emphasis on English

The history of rhetoric in American colleges, both within and outside of English departments, is also important background for understanding the history of writing program administration. This history also helps to explain why rhetoric was devalued and is still not particularly well understood in English departments, the academic home of many WPAs, and how what has become known as "current-traditional" rhetoric (first so named by Richard Young) developed and became so firmly established that it is still alive in some corners of academe.

The first book-length historical study involving rhetoric, Albert Kitzhaber's 1953 doctoral dissertation *(Rhetoric in American Colleges, 1850–1900)*, was not published until 1990, after circulating for years among scholars on microfilm and dog-eared photocopy. As John Gage details in the introduction to the book, it remains one of the most influential historical studies of the field. Kitzhaber gives a clear picture of how freshman composition began at Harvard and then spread throughout the country in the last half of the nineteenth century, thus creating a need for more persons to oversee the course. Prior to the Civil War, instruction in American universities was largely based on memorization and recitation, a pedagogical method designed to strengthen memory (and therefore useful to future clergyman); the student often memorized sections of a textbook and recited them aloud to his teacher (2). The teacher was more often than not a tutor, someone on the lowest rung of the academic ladder, and the teaching more often than not perfunctory (31). The purpose of education was to strengthen moral character through mental discipline, not to supply or create useful knowledge.

Kitzhaber points out that Charles W. Eliot is a key figure in the changes that took place at Harvard after 1869, changes that became the model for other institutions across the country (33). Eliot had himself studied in Germany, where many Americans went for doctoral study, and was a powerful force in establishing an elective system that encouraged specialization, introduced science into the curriculum, did away with recitation and substituted lectures, and most important for the history of language studies, raised the status of the modern languages, especially English, in place of the Greek and Latin of the classical curriculum. It was also during Eliot's presidency that entrance examinations began to be required, setting a precedent for similar exams at other institutions (and for WPA work to be forever intertwined with assessment). At first these examinations consisted of reading aloud (34), but soon concern for the written as well as the spoken word became apparent; by 1872 the Harvard catalog stated that correct spelling, punctuation, expression, and legible handwriting were expected of all applicants, and by 1873 a short composition (based on selections from English literature) was required (35). One of the reasons for the entrance requirement in English was to relegate the "mechanical" skills of writing to the preparatory schools, nearly all of which were still private,[3] so that the university could follow the German university model and devote itself to research. But of course, the students of yesteryear, like their counterparts today, did not always arrive at the university knowing how to write in the ways that their professors required. Mary Trachsel provides a full history of this first of many such exams in *Institutionalizing Literacy: The Historical Role of College Entrance Examinations in English*.

As James Berlin documents it in *Writing Instruction in Nineteenth-Century American Colleges*), the situation came to a head in 1891. The Harvard Board of Overseers appointed a committee of outside representatives from the professional world, who concluded that the preparatory schools were failing in their job and declared that teaching students how to write was not the college's concern—the lower schools must do a better job. The reports generated by the committee (the Harvard Reports of 1895 and 1897) were widely publicized, generating a series of "Why Johnny Can't Write" newspaper and magazine articles: "The larger effects of the Harvard Reports were unfortunate. Knowing nothing about writing instruction, the committee members focused on the most obvious features of the essays they read, the errors in spelling, grammar, usage, and even handwriting. They thus gave support to the view that has haunted writing classes: learning to write is learning matters of superficial correctness" (61). First year composition was born under the shadow of remediation and a focus on correctness, a heritage that can create difficulties for present-day writing program administrators.

The growth of first-year composition out of and then away from rhetoric is also documented by John Brereton in *The Origins of Composition Studies in the American College, 1875–1925: A Documentary History*. True to its title, this book reprints a number of original documents from the first composition program at Harvard and from subsequent programs at other institutions, as well as excerpts from early textbooks and various booklets and leaflets that instruct students about how to write essays and exams. For President Eliot, English was to be the modern equivalent of the classics, preparing students for citizenship and productive work in American democracy (9). To help carry out this new emphasis on English, Eliot had hired Adams

Sherman Hill, a newspaperman and lawyer, in 1872, making him Boylston Professor of Rhetoric in 1876. Hill was the force behind the first placement examination in English composition, forcing all preparatory schools to change their curricula to accommodate Harvard.[4] With the rise of discrete courses within particular disciplines, writing ceased to be a part of all classes across the curriculum (as David Russell has shown), and became confined to one course, a course that was gradually pushed down to the freshman year. As mentioned earlier, Harvard-trained students left to take teaching positions at other institutions, and other colleges began to develop a similar required course. John Michael Wozniak has traced the spread of first-year composition (as well as the accompanying transformation of traditional rhetoric into modern composition) by examining textbook adoptions at Eastern colleges. By 1900 the course was required nearly universally (Brereton *Origins* 13).[5]

Hill's influential text, *Principles of Rhetoric* (1878), took the stance that rhetoric was an art, not a science (Hill 321). Brereton argues that this was to be a devastating stance in an institution increasingly devoted to the scientific paradigm of research: "To argue that rhetoric was not a science, not a way of knowing, was to consign it to training, to an introductory level of college, to pedagogy. If it was an art, its instruction depended on the skill of the teacher, not on a knowledge base build up by concentrated study, by research" (*Origins* 10). Harvard's composition program depended on teachers, not scholars; it never developed a graduate program, after the fashion of other disciplines in the newly created research institutions, and did not develop the research that might have grounded the undergraduate program theoretically. The program, which had started with a group of talented faculty Brereton characterizes as true academic stars, began to lose its credibility even with the school's own faculty. And as Brereton points out, colleges have an unspoken rule: You are what you teach. "Working with first-year students is a job for a teacher, not a scholar. And of course since even its proponents argued it was an art, not a science, the notion grew that just about anyone could teach it, and before long just about anyone did. Even before teaching assistants were common, teaching composition was an entry level job, one to leave behind after acquiring seniority" (18). Rhetoric became the province of departments of speech or communication, where research was being done, not to be joined again to written composition until Edward P. J. Corbett published *Classical Rhetoric for the Modern Student* in 1965. The English department developed a system which prevails today: "professors teaching advanced literature courses, and instructors, part timers, and graduate students teaching composition. By 1910, composition had become almost totally apprentice work, and responsibility for its oversight became the province not of a scholar or curriculum expert but an administrator" (21), a bureaucratic functionary.

Development of a Composition Underclass

How composition teachers became an underclass in English departments is further detailed by Robert Connors ("Rhetoric in the Modern University"). The German research university, which had no undergraduate component, was the most advanced institution of its kind during the nineteenth century, attracting students from all over the world. Between 1815 and 1915 more than 10,000 Americans attended German universities (58); many of these, like Eliot, brought back not only new knowledge, but also a passionate enthusiasm for the research institution as a scholarly ideal, devoted to learning for learning's sake via empirical scientific investigation. Following Harvard's lead, American institutions began to be reorganized along the German model, with parallel specialties beginning to develop. But although there was a rich tradition of German research in the sciences and social sciences, there was no intellectual tradition of rhetoric in German universities—Americans going to Germany for doctorates came back as chemists, social scientists, mathematicians, psychologists, philologists, but not rhetoricians (62). As Connors notes,

> [i]n any bureaucracy, self-reproduction is necessary for institutional success and longevity. At this self-reproduction, the newly formed departments, including English, proved proficient. New graduate schools were founded in almost every year during the 1870s and 1880s, and soon new native PhDs were being sent into the world, charged by their teachers to be fruitful and multiply. The doctorate provided a convenient licensing structure for increasingly competitive graduate schools, and gradually, between 1880 and 1900, the PhD came to be seen as a *sine qua non*

> for prospective university (and even college) teachers.
>
> It was this demand for doctorates that truly spelled the end for rhetoric as a discipline [. . .]. ("Rhetoric in the Modern University" 63)

As early as the 1890s, composition began to be relegated to those Connors calls the "hapless bottom feeders": graduate students and instructors (72). These latter were usually in their last year of doctoral study; an instructorship was where a young PhD could expect to get started in order to rise through the ranks, a sort of apprenticeship system. These entry-level positions were the only ones available. But the research such students had been trained to do did not prepare them to teach composition, and new instructors were often assigned three, four, or five sections of composition per semester (sometimes when they were trying to finish their dissertations). It is no wonder, then, that these instructors came to hate teaching composition (73). With a few exceptions, "English departments decreed that literature teaching—the serious intellectual occupation of the discipline—would get the rewards. In fact, literature itself came to *be* the reward; a long apprenticeship in composition would be rewarded with literature teaching once promotion came" (Brereton, *Origins* 21–22). Further, a disproportionate number of these apprentice teachers were women. Of the limited opportunities for women to do graduate work at this time, most were in the humanities, especially in English. But academe was very much a male preserve. Women who entered the profession found it hard to rise above an entry-level position (77); they never reached the promised reward of teaching literature.

THE PEDAGOGY AND CURRICULA OF EARLY COMPOSITION COURSES

Because of the fact that composition was "apprentice work," the pedagogy developed accordingly into a formulaic approach that untrained (and usually unmotivated) teachers could take on immediately. Although determining prevailing pedagogy at any point in history involves some speculation (since teaching is an isolated and individual activity), we do have some reports that give us an indication of how the first composition courses at Harvard were taught. Hill himself seems to have been a somewhat ineffectual teacher, at least initially; Rollo Brown, in his biography of LeBaron Russell Briggs (one of the faculty Eliot hired in the early 1880s to assist Hill and who became Dean of the College) reports that at first Hill

> had no sense of discipline—as the word is used pedagogically—and the students, carrying on the easy traditions of a course that had been under the direction of young men who taught transiently, were not inclined to look upon his work with overmuch seriousness. In truth, they sometimes hummed pleasant academic melodies while he read a man's theme in the classroom. (51)

However, he persisted, and by the early 1880s Eliot hired colleagues to assist him: Barrett Wendell, W. B. Shubrick Clymer, and Briggs. The pedagogy by this point seems to have been adversarial, "with the teacher as a stern taskmaster skilled in rooting out falsehood and cant and the student in fear of the teacher's scorn" (Brereton *Origins* 19). Wendell in particular seems to have been a quirky individual and teacher, as detailed by Wallace Douglas in his essay "Barrett Wendell," affecting what his students called "eccentricities of voice and manner" (8).

One mode of instruction was clearly lecture; Barrett Wendell put together a textbook based on his own composition course, *English Composition: Eight Lectures Given at The Lowell Institute* (1891), and subsequently used by others for their courses. The collected lectures take an atomistic approach to teaching writing, focusing on words, sentences, and paragraphs, then on the whole composition in terms of unity, form, coherence, and style (clearness, force, and aesthetic elegance), an approach that may still be found in some modern composition textbooks. Wendell did launch an important pedagogical innovation for the course, the "daily theme," an exercise evidently based on his own practice of daily writing and designed to help students be more accurate observers of the world around them (R. Brown 57) and one that became a hallmark of first-year composition at Harvard. He also required students to read and criticize each others' themes in class, focusing on the subject of each chapter in his book: first on words, then sentences, then paragraphs, and finally style. Wendell comments that this approach is useful for two reasons: "In categorically criticising the theme of somebody else, [the student] is compelled at once intelligently to master the theory of the chapter under consideration, and to display his knowledge of it in an orderly way. And if he criticises well—which proves the case rather oftener than one would expect—he greatly lightens the task of the instructor who has finally to criticise the theme in question" (2).

The demand for information about how the "daily theme" composition course at Harvard was run became so great that two of the people teaching it published a book that set forth the methods of the course: Copeland and Rideout's *Freshman English and Theme Correcting in Harvard College*. The authors state that in 1899–1900 this course was taught in a scale that was evidently larger than most: 620 or so students taught in 19 sections by 11 different instructors, but the scheme could be modified for smaller groups. In the introduction to the book they offer their explanation of the course, that it "might suggest something practical to one who is attempting to attain for himself or to impart to others a simple and adequate prose style" since "this, the habitual use of correct and intelligent English, is what the instructors try to drill into the Freshmen" (2). The point of the class is to train a group of young men, some of whom the authors termed "illiterate" and some of whom were more mature writers, "to the point where they can write English of which they need not be ashamed" (2). The daily themes were key to this objective: Copeland and Rideout are clear that the "first effort of the instructors [. . .] is not to make the daily themes interesting, but to make them correct" (9).

To accomplish the task of writing error-free prose, students were to provide themselves with Prof. Adam Sherman Hill's revised *Principles of Rhetoric*[6] as a text, along with an English Composition Card, which gave them a key to the abbreviations for the corrections they were to make on their themes. Just how well faculty actually followed this key in responding to students is cause for speculation. In his biography of Briggs, Rollo Brown states that at a dinner in honor of the great man at the Harvard Club in 1925, a student rose and addressed him:

> "We have always wanted to know more about those WWWs, YUUs, and WBZs and the like that you used to put on the outside of our stories. Now that you are through using them, we should like to be let in on the secret. What are they? And what do they mean?" Dean Briggs arose, smiling to the top of his

head, and replied: "They are private symbols I devised for indicating the quality of themes. They don't mean anything except to me!" (91n)

The writing assignments were fortnightly themes (three to six pages) that had to be rewritten or at least revised, daily themes (some of which were translations) of not more than one page (which also had to be revised if "faulty" [3]), and readings from various literary texts as well as from Hill. Students were also required to attend three lectures or recitations per week, one of which was the "third hour" general meeting of multiple sections (according to Brown, this was added when Professors Hill and Briggs insisted that the class should be upgraded to a three-hour class, and the senior faculty agreed to add it only if it did not require any work outside the classroom [54]), confer with his instructor once a month, memorize 50 lines from a prescribed text, and read "one or two prescribed books, of which he is expected to form an intelligent opinion" (6). There were also mid-term and final examinations, with options for instructors to hold hourly examinations if needed. The authors provide a helpful outline of the course, the first example we have of a document that has become an important part of modern WPA work, the curriculum guide for a multi-section course (see Figure 1).

The impact of this pedagogy seems to have been widespread at the beginning; Rollo Brown tells us that "teachers in hundreds of colleges wanted to know more about this method of helping men to see clearly and write directly. Newspaper editors rejoiced that college men were learning to write straight sentences; and magazines and weeklies discussed the educational value of the 'daily theme' eye" (58). Further, Brown tells us that Wendell and his colleagues "trained men to look at the world with their own eyes, and to write directly and honestly about what they saw, without regard for the traditional ways of looking at things. The men thus trained went all over the country to teach in the colleges and universities, and they carried with the gospel that the world right where one lives is interesting if one will only look and think" (59). The curriculum developed at Harvard by these early faculty lasted from 1875–1910.

But as Brereton documents, the Harvard approach was not without its critics. Many institutions were developing alternatives. The first was simply to set the entrance requirements high and have no writing classes at all; a few colleges (like Princeton) made this alternative

	DAILY THEMES	FORTNIGHTLY THEMES	EXAMINATIONS	READING[1]	MEETINGS AND CONFERENCES
October	Subjects taken from observation of surroundings. Translations once a week. "Third-hour" themes. Special exercises in class.	Oct. 25. Theme I.: "Who I Am, and Why I Came to Harvard." Due rewritten or revised, as all other fortnightly themes, within two weeks.		"King Henry IV.," Part I., or "Antony and Cleopatra," or "Twelfth Night."	
November	As in October.	Nov. 8. Theme II.: "How to Make or Do Something." Nov. 22. Theme III.: "Something Learned in a College Course."	An examination, one hour long, at the discretion of the instructor.	Mr. Kipling: "The Jungle Book."	
December	Weekly translations. "Third-hour" themes. Special exercises in class. No restriction as to the subjects of other daily themes.	Dec. 6. Theme IV.: "An Expression of Opinion on some Topic of Interest." Dec. 22. Theme V.: No subject prescribed. A criticism of one of the "required" books recommended.		Thackeray: "Pendennis," or (for those who have read "Pendennis") "Henry Esmond," or "Vanity Fair."	Every week: Two lectures or recitations in each "section" of about thirty men; one meeting of several united sections, with lectures and writing of "third-hour" themes.
January	As in December, with the addition of Invitations, Letters of Acceptance, etc.	Jan. 17. Theme VI.: A Biographical Portrait.	The midyear examination (three hours).		
February	As in December.	Feb. 28. Theme VII.: A Description.		Macaulay: Life of Clive, or Life of Johnson, or Life of Hastings.	Every month: One conference, — an interview, for fifteen minutes, between student and instructor.
March	As in December.	March 14. Theme VIII.: A Description. March 28. Theme IX.: A Narrative.			
April	As in December.	April 11. Theme X.: A Narrative.	An hour examination, at the discretion of the instructor.	George Eliot: "Adam Bede."	
May	As in December.	May 7. Theme XI.: A Brief. May 23. Theme XII.: An Argument.			
June			The final examination (three hours).		

[1] Throughout the year the students read Professor Hill's "Principles of Rhetoric." They also read one book of "The Golden Treasury," and commit to memory fifty lines from the Fourth Book.

Figure 1. "Outline for Freshman English at Harvard, 1899–1900." From C. T. Copeland and H. M. Rideout, *Freshman English and Theme Correcting at Harvard College.* New York: Silver Burdett, 1901 (pp. 4–5).

work for a long time (*Origins* 14). There were also notable exceptions to the Harvard model developed by dedicated individuals, as Susan Kates documents in *Activist Rhetorics and American Higher Education, 1885–1937.* Kates describes the pedagogy at three institutions founded in the late nineteenth and early twentieth century to serve the disenfranchised (middle-class white women at Smith College, African American women at Wilberforce University, and the working classes at Brookwood Labor College) that emphasized the relationship between language and identity, addressed civic issues, and brought community service into the curriculum. But as Brereton documents, what eventually displaced the Harvard system at most institutions was "an eclectic mix of three other approaches: personal writing, writing about literature, and writing about ideas" (*Origins* 15). Personal writing, adapted from Wendell's daily themes, focused on personal experience; at Michigan, Fred Newton Scott argued for such a curriculum as a way to connect writing to real experience, and Scott's student Gertrude Buck "wrote articles that provided some of the most sensible rationale for this kind of writing . . . and wrote a text embodying it" (15). The composition course that focuses on literature as a basis for writing actually predated the Harvard approach, invented and popularized by Thomas Lounsbury at Yale—an elective course in literature that had a heavy writing requirement (16). This sort of course became extremely popular, given the fact that English department faculty could draw upon their own expertise in literature. There were many variations of the course, all of which involved "some elements of the old rhetoric course's emphasis on *belles lettres*, style, and examples drawn from English literature. In the most common type of literature-based course students read a wide variety of English (and later, American) works: poems, some plays, plus a novel or two, and write critical essays about them" (16). A third alternative was what Brereton terms "the idea course," which became popular after the turn of the century. This course consisted of a close analysis of literary non-fiction essays with the emphasis on the structure of ideas (16). It was first taught by Frank Aydelotte at Indiana in the 1890s; Aydelotte wrote about the course in several national journals (one particularly influential one published in *Educational Review* was entitled "English as Training in Thought"). He also wrote a textbook entitled *College English,* designed to help teachers organize a course combining literature and composition as he had done at Indiana. Although the course did not survive at

Indiana, his textbook seems to have had considerable influence on the curricula of other institutions, in particular Wisconsin and Columbia (Blanchard 111). Brereton states that this course "developed into the most common of all early twentieth-century composition courses, the expository writing course stressing certain key works of serious nonfiction. Students would analyze the prose and sometimes react to its ideas, at other times imitate its structure or style" (*Origins* 17). By 1920,

> composition had assumed the shape it would retain for the next half century [. . .]. The half-century from 1875 to 1925 had witnessed an enormous revolution in the relation of composition to students and to other academic subjects, all within the context of a transformation of America higher education. It is not surprising that this period of ferment should have been followed by a period of stasis[[. . .]. Composition, like much in the American Curriculum, had become stable, at a point very far away from the rhetoric of the 1850s. (25)

A sort of canon of essays developed for the class, embodied in a rhetoric/reader textbook, sometimes accompanied by a handbook; this approach became identified with what has become known as "current-traditional rhetoric."

THE TENACITY OF CURRENT-TRADITIONAL RHETORIC[7]

Given the underclass status of composition and the lack of a scholarly tradition to inform the development of a curriculum or scholars to oversee it, it is not surprising that the composition curriculum and its pedagogy became formulaic. The term to describe this approach, "current-traditional rhetoric," was first proposed by Richard Young in his 1978 essay, "Paradigms and Problems: Needed Research in Rhetorical Invention," borrowing the term from Daniel Fogerty's *Roots for a New Rhetoric* (and adding a hyphen). As Young describes it, the features of this approach are familiar: "The emphasis on the composed product rather than the composing process; the analysis of discourse into description, narration, exposition, and argument; the strong concern with usage (syntax, spelling, punctuation) and with style (economy, clarity, emphasis); the preoccupation with the informal essay and the research paper; and so on" (31). The rise of this approach to teaching composition, which (as Young noted) included teaching the "modes" of discourse (exposition, description, narration, and argument, or EDNA, as Sharon Crowley has termed them in *The Methodical Memory* [101]), was first discussed by Kitzhaber and then chronicled more fully by Robert Connors in "The Rise and Fall of the Modes of Discourse" and in "The Rhetoric of Explanation: Explanatory Rhetoric from 1850 to the Present." Although an approach focusing on four modes of discourse has waned, as Connors notes, the formulaic and arhetorical nature of current-traditional rhetoric is still alive in many texts and programs. The history of current-traditional rhetoric is therefore important for an understanding of the history of writing program administration.

Connors traces the development of the modes in various textbooks published in the nineteenth century, especially the 1866 textbook *English Composition and Rhetoric* by Scottish logician and educator Alexander Bain. Up until Bain's text, most American composition textbooks were organized around belletristic kinds of discourse (sermons, treatises, history, orations, etc.). Although the "four modes" had been mentioned in earlier texts, Bain made them the organizing principle of his book. Connors describes briefly how Bain posited three "departments" of the mind—Understanding, Will, and Feelings—and developed the modes around them. The classification scheme was then picked up by John Genung (a Baptist minister with a German PhD who spent his teaching career at Amherst), who published several textbooks, the most influential of which was *Outlines of Rhetoric* published in 1893. (A comprehensive treatment of textbooks from this period may be found in Carr, Carr, and Schultz, *Archives of Instruction: Nineteenth-Century Rhetorics, Readers, and Composition Books in the United States.*) By 1895 the modes were entrenched textbooks and therefore in the classroom. As Connors tells the story, pedagogy based on the modes waxed strong during the enormous changes taking place in rhetorical study during the latter half of the nineteenth century, and only began to wane in the mid twentieth century. Connors notes that the persistence of the modes should be taken as a warning:

> For years the fact that this schema did not help students learn to write better was not a concern, and even today the modes are accepted by some teachers

> despite their lack of basis in useful reality. Our discipline has been long in knuckling from its eyes the sleep of the nineteenth and early twentieth centuries, and the real lesson of the modes is that we need always to be on guard against systems that seem convenient to teachers but that ignore the way writing is actually done. ("Rise" 455)

One of the reasons that the modes "lack a basis in useful reality" is the fact that the scheme is grounded in nineteenth-century theories of psychology (then called "mental philosophy"). William Woods points out in "Nineteenth-Century Psychology and the Teaching of Writing" that these theories were of necessity speculative rather than empirical (21); they were not systems identified with particular theorists, but general assumptions that shaped the thinking of a number of early psychologists, and which influenced Alexander Bain as he developed his composition textbooks. Woods explains that there were two lines of explanation for the way the human mind worked: one theory held that there were innate "faculties" (such as memory or taste) that could explain human thought, feelings, and will. The other held that individual (or "simple") ideas coming from memory or immediate sensory data were combined according to "principles of association" to form complex ideas and groups of ideas. Woods points out that these two lines of thought were mutually exclusive. "The 'faculty' theories did make limited use of the principle of association in their treatment of memory, but the associationists utterly rejected the theory of the faculties of mind, even though they would sometimes use its terminology (the will, the feelings, etc.), as we still do, for the sake of convenience" (21). Bain, as did other progressive thinkers of the 1800s, held with associationist theories.

In "The Intellectual Background of Alexander Bain's 'Modes of Discourse,'" Jon Harned explores more fully the question of why Bain focused on the modes as he did, showing how Bain's approach was grounded in the scientific thought of the day and his contributions to it in his own writings, especially *The Senses and the Intellect*. Bain posited what are essentially two laws: the law of contiguity, when actions or feelings that occur together cohere so that to remember one is to remember the others, and the law of similarity, when actions or feelings revive previous similar actions or feelings (43–44). Bain went on to apply these laws to rhetoric, positing that various figures of speech appealed to three forms of mental activity: thought, will, and feeling.

> It is by means of these three sorts of rhetorical appeals that Bain classifies the modes of discourse. Description, Narration, and Exposition address the Understanding; Persuasion (or Oratory, as he sometimes calls it), and Poetry addresses the Feelings. The conception of Description, Narration, and Exposition as modes of discourse derives from the laws of association, though Bain never says so explicitly. "Description" exercises the associative operation of contiguity in which the world is perceived frozen in time like a still life [. . .]. "Narration"
>
> [. . .] is the perception of contiguity in time, of the world in flux [. . .]. "Exposition" as a form of writing is based on the discovery of similarity, and is linked in Bain's mind, like the Law of Similarity, with science. (Harned 45–46)

Harned points to one of the reasons that Bain's taxonomy of discourse became so popular and so lasting. At the time he wrote it, American education was undergoing a transformation—the small liberal arts college was on the decline, and the modern university with its focus on research and on graduate and professional schools was emerging. The modes of discourse were a better fit than the old belletristic forms for this new kind of institution, since they had to do not with aesthetics but with the business of communication, and since they could present themselves as scientific (48). James Berlin, in *Writing Instruction in Nineteenth-Century American Colleges,* also argues that the rise of the modes signals the triumph of the "scientific approach," one that was not successfully challenged until the mid-twentieth century (62).

This is one reason why, over time, the modes of discourse began to collapse into what Bain thought of as the most "scientific" of them, exposition. In "The Rhetoric of Explanation," Robert Connors describes more fully this gradual narrowing of the writing curriculum. The beginnings of a movement towards an emphasis on exposition, Connors argues, was Henry Day's 1850 text *Elements of the Art of Rhetoric* (published in a second edition as *The Art of Discourse,* 1867). Day's analysis of explanatory discourse presents the first version of the "methods of exposition" that became so common in later textbooks: narration, description, analysis, exemplification, and comparison and contrast. The popularity of Bain's *English Composition and Rhetoric* during the latter half of the nineteenth century eclipsed Day's work, but exposition experienced a revival as a result of an 1893 text written by Fred Newton Scott and Joseph V. Denney, *Paragraph Writing.* For quite some time, separate textbooks had been appearing for each of the four modes; as English and speech began to break apart into separate disciplines, argumentation went with speech. There was a slow rise of a renewed version of Day's processes of explanation; then, the text Connors calls the "watershed" book appeared: *Expository Writing* by Maurice Garland Fulton. Fulton was not a theoretician, but someone Connors describes as a functionary given to the creation of anthologies who happened to hit it big. In the introduction to his text, Fulton said that he wished to "centre attention upon exposition since it is the kind of writing that is most directly serviceable in practical life" (v). Connors tells us that after 1912 the history of written rhetoric is essentially that of the waxing of expository writing. One of the reasons for its popularity was that it provided a "neatly packaged and easily taught pedagogical tool, a tool of a sort no other mode offered" (64).

> It is sad but true to say that there was no real rhetorical theory attached to explanation. The pedagogy worked itself out in textbooks according to laws of the marketplace and cultural stimuli; nothing new or innovative was propounded. It was not until the early 1960s, when composition studies began to shake off the lethargy that had long been associated with its second-class status within English departments, that we again see a vital scholarly tradition in explanatory rhetoric, a tradition that had been missing since the death of Fred Scott. (67)

The fact that associationist and faculty theories of how the mind worked were mutually exclusive did not deter current-traditional pedagogy from using them both. Faculty psychology held that mental processes were a result of innate "faculties" such as memory, will, taste, judgment (the list varied); the theory held that there was an analogy between the powers of the mind and the powers of the body. Exercising a muscle and it grows stronger; ergo, exercise the will, judgment, taste, memory, etc., and those faculties will become stronger as well. Since these are general faculties, it follows that exercising them will improve performance in other areas: exercising the memory in memorization of grammar rules will help develop a practical grasp of other details, useful in, say, business or law. Memorization of grammar rules is not only an aid to mental discipline, it is a form of self-improvement (Woods 22–23); thus grammar drills became embedded in the teaching of writing not for the sake of improving writing, but for the sake of exercising students' minds and strengthening their moral fiber.

It is not surprising that faculty as well as associationist psychology should have such an influence on writing pedagogy, since it was consonant with the educational theories of the time. In *The American School 1642–1985,* Joel Spring points out that in the early part of the nineteenth century Americans organized a number of different institutions, including schools, for the moral reformation of society; there was a widespread belief in the power of these institutions to perfect the good person, which would then create the good society (47). Nineteenth-century theories of psychology were key to the notion of character malleability through schooling. The educational theories of Benjamin Rush (the "father of American psychiatry" according to Spring) were particularly influential, since he argued that a moral faculty was a natural part of the human mind (48). Faculty psychology in general reflected the growing belief in the early part of the nineteenth century that human beings were perfectible. "This belief provided the intellectual basis for the reform movements in the early part of the nineteenth century that produced modern systems of education and other institutions designed to improve human character" (49).

The guiding standard for many colleges in this regard was the Yale Report of 1828, a report that was a reaction against some of the curricular reforms then being proposed. This report, among other things, sets out the basis for some aspects of college life that persisted up until very recently: the need for *in loco parentis* control of students to protect them from temptation, the resulting necessity for residential schooling, and most importantly, a curriculum that provided a general background of knowledge that provided a balanced exercise of the mental faculties. If any mental faculty were not exercised, the mind would not achieve full perfection (Yale Report, 63–64).

> The reasoning used in the report was that balanced mental faculties would result in a balanced charac-

ter. The general studies offered by the college were to provide the exercise necessary for achieving a balance of mental faculties and character [. . .]. Each subject-matter area would contribute to the exercise of a different part of the mind. For instance, the report claims that mathematics would teach demonstrative reasoning, physical sciences would teach inductive reasoning, ancient literature would provide finished models of taste, English reading would teach speaking and writing, philosophy would teach thinking, and rhetoric and oratory would teach the art of speaking. (65)

In *The Emergence of the American University,* Laurence Veysey points out that this view of education was entirely consonant with the view of colleges founded on a religious base. He quotes from James McCosh's inaugural address as president of Princeton in 1868: "I hold it to be the highest end of a University to *educate;* that is, to draw out and improve the faculties which God has given. Our Creator, no doubt, means all things in our world to be perfect in the end; but he has not made them perfect; he has left room for growth and progress; and it is a task laid on his intelligent creatures to be fellow-workers with him in finishing that work which he has left incomplete" (23).

Thus the entire curriculum of the university in pre-Civil War times was based on the theories of faculty psychology. Although the curriculum changed radically in the late nineteenth century, the Yale Report (and with it, theories of faculty psychology) continued to set the tone for collegiate education well into the twentieth century; it can still be detected in some current conversations about what constitutes a liberal education and what the outcomes of general education programs should be. It is no wonder, then, that the modes of discourse and the focus on grammar in the teaching of writing have enjoyed such long life. With no scholarly tradition and few researchers/scholars to head up writing programs, the teaching of composition remained fixed for generations in formulaic approaches determined by textbook writers.

The Pre-Professional Period: Writing Program Administration up to World War II

Barbara L'Eplattenier argues that two factors argue for the pre-1940s existence of the work, if not the title, of writing program administrators: "First is the sheer size of Freshman or Introductory Composition at most institutions and the ways these immense programs were organized; second is recent historical work about women, historical work that has tangentially uncovered women working as writing program administrators within First-Year Composition programs" ("Finding" 133).

Let us first consider size. Although the growing size of the student body during the period before World War II was not nearly at the rate that it would be after the G.I. Bill, the increases were still considerable. As John Heyda notes, in 1870 there were 52,000 students enrolled in all institutions of higher education in the United States. A decade later the figure had risen by 131 percent to 116,000. During the 1880s it rose another 35 percent, in the 1890s by 50 percent, in the first decade of the twentieth century by 68 percent, and by 1930 to 1,101,000 ("Industrial-Strength Composition" 251). Although the depression of the 1930s slowed growth for a time, by 1940 nationwide totals had risen to 1,494,000. As enrollments soared, universities had to develop institutional structures to manage them, especially since the size of the faculty did not increase proportionately.[8]

During this period, writing program administration was, to use David Schwalm's distinction (see Chapter 2), a task rather than a position. Because there were not yet professional organizations for WPAs, the history of writing program administration during the period from the beginning of first-year composition up to World War II is necessarily a history of individuals assigned to that task in individual programs. We have few such histories; as Joseph V. Denney wrote in 1897, "composition work is in theory the business of everybody and in reality the business of nobody" (6). However, Barbara L'Eplattenier argues that the administrative histories we do have "demonstrate that the work of writing program administration has existed as long as there have been institutions offering writing courses" ("Finding" 136). Both Charles Pain (*The Resistant Writer: Rhetoric as Immunity, 1850 to the Present*) and Randall Popkin ("Edwin Hopkins and the Costly Labor of Composition Teaching") argue for a biographical approach to the early history of composition, stating that broad ideological studies have limited usefulness; we should also be looking at the relationship between a person's life and his or her pedagogy and professional contributions. Such an "historical case study" approach seems particularly useful in considering the early history of writing program administration. In reviewing these individual histories, however, it is important to avoid what historians refer to as "presentism," which Hunt (in the online version of the American Historical Association's newsletter) defines as "the tendency to interpret the past in present terms." It is important to keep in mind the social and historical context in which these persons worked, and that our own views of students and of composition were probably not their views, even though some of the administrative work they carried out was similar.

In the period before World War I there are a few rhetoricians whose work has been studied in some detail; Kitzhaber lists these as "The Big Four": Adams Sherman Hill and Barrett Wendell at Harvard, John Franklin Genung at Amherst, and Fred Newton Scott at the University of Michigan (59–73). All were teachers of writing and authors of influential textbooks, but Kitzhaber states that only Scott was an original thinker; because he also chaired a separate department of rhetoric, we may also think of him as a writing program administrator. Scott's contributions are discussed in Kitzhaber's *Rhetoric in American Colleges, 1850–1900* (and Berlin, following Kitzhaber, in *Writing Instruction in Nineteenth-Century American Colleges*), Brereton's *The Origins of Composition Studies in the American College, 1875–1925,* and, most fully, in a series of articles by Donald Stewart and in *The Life and Legacy of Fred Newton Scott* by Donald and Patricia Stewart. Scott spent his entire career, both as a student and as a faculty member, at Michigan: he received his BA in 1884, his MA in 1888, his PhD in 1889, and was a faculty member from 1889 until he retired in 1927 (Kitzhaber 70). His interest in rhetoric was keen; in fact, Kitzhaber notes that even though the term "rhetoric" was out of favor, he insisted on being known by the title "Professor of Rhetoric" rather than of English (70). Scott is particularly interesting because he was an exception to the rule of non-scholarly writing program administration in his time.

Scott was evidently an incredibly energetic, even charismatic leader on the national level: he served at one time or another as the President of the Modern Language Association, as President of the National Council of Teachers of English, as President of the North Central Association of Colleges and Secondary schools, and as President of the American Association of Journalism Teachers (Stewart "Rediscovering Fred Newton Scott"). His leadership in his own institution was also strong; in 1903, apparently because of his request, the university set up a separate Department of Rhetoric, with Scott himself at the helm. This department included creative writing and journalism, courses in the fundamental principles of rhetoric and criticism, courses designed for students who were preparing to teach, and courses to give students practice with the leading types of prose composition. As Stewart and Stewart demonstrate, the description of the courses offered during its first year demonstrate that this was a total program, balancing theory and practice, endorsing a generous definition of rhetoric that included historical, theoretical, and practical work (41), quite different from the curriculum at Harvard. Perhaps most important, the department developed a graduate program in rhetoric, producing some distinguished graduates (such as Gertrude Buck) who went on to leadership roles at other institutions.

In "A Model for Our Time: Fred Newton Scott's Rhetoric Program at Michigan," Stewart defines Scott as a model in terms of his expansive notion of rhetoric. Although he does not go as far as Berlin in characterizing him as an early social constructionist, Stewart does detail Scott's insistence on rhetoric in a social context. Both Stewart and Berlin agree that "Scott was shaping an alternative to the dominant current-traditional rhetoric of the time" (Stewart "Model" 43). In collaboration with Joseph V. Denney and with his own former student Gertrude Buck, Scott wrote a number of textbooks on rhetoric that gave teachers alternatives to the dominant pedagogical approach of the time and for twenty years edited a series of research publications (under the general heading of *Contributions to Rhetorical Theory*) that gave his graduate students an outlet for their work with him (Kitzhaber 71–72). As many writing program administrators do today, he worked to establish good relationships with the preparatory schools in Michigan:

> At Harvard, where secondary school English was looked on with something not far from contempt, teachers of English in the schools were blamed for all the linguistic shortcomings of entering freshmen. Scott took a different approach. He tried to reduce the gap between the high school teacher and the col-

> lege teacher, to show that both had essentially the same problems. For years he labored to bring about cooperation and understanding for the benefit of both groups. He was in thorough agreement with the plan that had established a pyramidal educational structure in Michigan, with the elementary schools at the base and the university at the apex, each level having responsibilities toward the others. He called it the "organic" plan, as opposed to the "feudal plan" followed by Harvard. (Kitzhaber 72)

Unfortunately, Scott's model of writing instruction and also of writing program administration did not prevail during this period. Stewart details this story of Scott and his program in "Two Model Teachers and the Harvardization of English Departments." In this essay Stewart describes the Harvard approach as embodied by Francis Child, Harvard's fourth Boylston Professor of Rhetoric. During the years he held that title, Child had complained bitterly about the years he had wasted correcting freshman themes. Stewart states that he was "absorbed in his own research. The kind of contact with students that rhetoric requires could only have irritated him. In fact, Albert Bushnell Hart wrote that 'Francis Child used to say with a disarming twinkle that the university would never be perfect until we got rid of all the students' " (qtd. in Stewart,120). He was delighted when in 1876 Johns Hopkins, the first American university to be established on the German research university model, offered him a chair in English literature. Harvard, unwilling to lose him, created a similar chair for him and moved his assistant, Adams Sherman Hill, into the Boylston Professorship. Child was determined to elevate the status of literature study to an academic discipline; from 1872 to 1910 he seems to have almost single-handedly built an English department, one that (because of the prestige and influence of Harvard) became the model for departments all over the country—a model that still survives.

Stewart tells this story as one of professional choice: "In the late nineteenth century the young profession of English came to a fork in the road, and with little hesitation, I suspect, made its choice and confidently set out on a path with which it was and has been fully comfortable" (119). As Connors points out, it was "a rattling good story, and certain ways it is even an accurate one. But it is not the complete story, and work in composition history since 1985 has been struggling to add some depth to the all-too-simple tale of Decline and Fall." One of the problems with this Harvardization tale is that it "does not look deeply enough into the social, cultural, and ideological contexts of rhetoric and composition as they developed in their own eras" ("History" 64).

One important piece of contextual information for Scott's story was resources, as Brereton makes clear. Even though Michigan's was the most comprehensive writing program in the country, it was shockingly short on faculty even during the time that it was part of the English Department; in 1895 Scott was one of four full-time faculty responsible for teaching 1,200 students a year (*Origins* 177). During the period between the two world wars Michigan, like other universities, was experiencing burgeoning enrollments; in 1900–01, a total of 3,712 students were enrolled, but by 1920–21 there were 10,623, with no substantial increase in resources to teach them. In 1923 the Rhetoric Department enrolled 2,600 students, 1,513 of whom were freshmen. Composition classes averaged about 30 students (Stewart and Stewart 171). The enrollments became larger than the administrative structure could sustain. It is also clear that Scott's program was not the only separate department of rhetoric created only to disappear some years later; Scott's friend Edwin Hopkins created a separate unit at Kansas at about the same time (see below), Mount Holyoke and Wellesley also had separate departments for rhetoric (L'Eplattenier and Mastrangelo 140), and in a 1908–09 internal report, the chair of Vassar's English department states that dividing departments into two units, rhetoric and literature, "has been unfortunately done in many places" (Bordelon 104). The demise of these separate units focusing on rhetoric coincided with and was related to the rise of separate departments of speech. A final issue was the great energy of Scott himself. The department of Rhetoric *was* Scott, and under his leadership it flourished for thirty years. But it flourished only as long as his energy could sustain it as a one-man show; there was no institutional or professional structure to sustain it. Two years after his retirement, the department was absorbed back into English and sank without a trace.[9] Scott's story is an object lesson for the profession; unless they are institutionalized in some way, programs that depend on the energy and resourcefulness of only one WPA are only as strong and long-lived as that person.

The career of Edward Hopkins is discussed in "The WPA as Publishing Scholar: Edwin Hopkins and *The Labor and Cost of the Teaching of English*" and "Edward Hopkins and the Costly Labor of Composition Teaching," both by Randall Popkin; Hopkins's career provides us with an early model of the writing program administrator as researcher. Hopkins (1892–1946) taught at the University of Kansas his entire career and was a founding member of the National Council of Teachers of English. He knew Fred Newton Scott, and like Scott (perhaps using the Michigan model) lobbied for a separate program. In 1902 the Department of English Literature, Language, and *Belles Lettres* was divided into a Department of English Literature and a Department of Rhetoric and English Language (which consisted mostly of first-year rhetoric classes), with Hopkins as chair of the latter. Thus his position, like Scott's, in some ways resembled that of today's WPA.

As Popkin notes, although Hopkins published work on the teaching of literature and composition, he is best known for the research project that resulted in a book that was the first of its kind: *The Labor and Cost of the Teaching of English in Colleges and Secondary Schools, with Especial Reference to English Composition,* published by NCTE in 1923; it was an empirical study of the workload of composition teachers, a topic that still resonates with WPAs today. It became a bestseller and a famous piece of scholarship, one that sought to prove that there were serious difficulties for faculty when they had too many students to teach. His research gives us some notion of the conditions of the time: faculty he surveyed had an average of 104.1 students per semester, and most found it impossible to do their work well. He argued that, based on his calculations, a reasonable student load for each faculty member would ideally be 36 students, but that an absolute maximum would be 62. Popkin argues that Hopkins' research provides an early model for WPA work as scholarship, making recommendations for program improvement that are grounded in research (like his study of class size and workload). His own history as a WPA is also cautionary. Popkin documents the fact that Hopkins himself had an almost impossible schedule as a teacher and writing program administrator, at one time needing a year's sick leave for illness and nervous exhaustion.

Most of these individual histories of WPAs are from research institutions. Kenneth Lindbloom and Patricia Dunn argue that one of the reasons for the dominance of what they call the "Harvard narrative" in the history of composition studies is the focus on research which has fostered disrespect for pedagogy as well as for administration; the history of those institutions whose mission it was to produce teachers—the normal schools—has been left out of the story (37–38). They trace the story of a cooperative program at one such institution, Illinois State Normal University, from 1904–1905, and in particular the influence of one professor, J. Rose Colby (who was the first person to receive an English PhD from the University of Michigan in 1886, three years ahead of Fred Newton Scott). According to manuscripts in the school's archives, Prof. Colby believed that schooling, especially the study of language, had both social and ethical purposes; she believed that language study belonged not just in English classes but across the curriculum (41). The authors trace her work on a "Committee on English" from 1904–1905, a committee whose recommendations focuses on asking content area teachers to take more responsibility for student writing; they state that this might be seen as "an early call for writing across the curriculum" (49). As a corrective to any "presentism," however, the authors note that part of Prof. Colby's motivation was to free literature teachers from the demands of language instruction (60).

Recent feminist projects to include women in the histories of rhetoric and composition, as noted above by L'Eplattenier, have shed some light on the histories of other women involved in writing program development and/or administration. During the late nineteenth century a number of women's colleges were founded, serving the daughters of the rising middle class (as Solomon's study of women's colleges at the end of the nineteenth century shows, the rich still educated their daughters at home). The most prominent of these were the "Seven Sisters" institutions: Barnard (1889), Bryn Mawr (1885), Mt. Holyoke (1837), Radcliffe (1879), Smith (1871), Vassar (1861), and Wellesley (1870). Since Harvard is so central to the story of first-year composition, one might think that Radcliffe would be as well; but Radcliffe was an anomaly among women's colleges. Although Harvard began admitting women in the late nineteenth century, they were not admitted on the same basis as men but as part of the Harvard Annex. This unit opened in 1879 as Radcliffe College, but as JoAnn Campbell points out, Radcliffe "had no college buildings, no dormitory life for its women students, and the professors were all Harvard faculty who offered the women their lectures and courses for pay in addition to their Harvard salaries. Even after there were dormitories, only men taught the students" ("Controlling" 476). It is to the separate women's institutions that we must look for the histories of women WPAs.

Of these, perhaps the most distinguished was Gertrude Buck, who spent her entire career at Vassar College. Buck was a student of Fred Newton Scott, receiving her PhD from the University of Michigan in rhetoric in 1898 (the first such degree in the U.S.). Brereton discusses Buck's contributions to the writing curricula of the time; taking Scott's argument for personal themes to connect writing to real experience, Buck wrote articles "that provided some of the most sensible rationale for this kind of writing" (*Origins* 15). Brereton reproduces a 1901 article by Buck, published in the *Educational Review*, "Recent Tendencies in the Teaching of English Composition," that sets forth this rationale, arguing for an alternative to the Harvard approach of composition without an academic subject matter (*Origins* 241–51). As well as critical and theoretical articles, Buck also published co-authored textbooks on composition that set forth the innovative curricula she developed at Vassar. In *Toward a Feminist Rhetoric: The Writing of Gertrude Buck* (a useful collection of Buck's work), JoAnn Campbell argues that Buck's writings show an effort to "rethink a patriarchal rhetorical tradition, reshape teacher-centered classrooms, and revise intellectual and social issues of concern to women" (ix). The descriptions of the pedagogy she developed to go with her co-authored textbook, *A Course in Expository Writing* (1899), would seem to bear out this claim. There were few lectures and no quizzes (since these were considered not to be compatible with free discussion); instead there were discussions of the literature they had read, individual and group interviews with the teacher on the themes they had written, and group work in class for discussing and critiquing themes. In 1917 a publication called *The Sampler* was inaugurated, in which students could publish their work (*Toward* xxxi), providing the "real audience" that Buck argued was the way to encourage students to critique their own work carefully (*Course* v). Buck's writings challenged the contemporary reductive view of writing as grammar instruction; her focus on grammar was holistic and logical and her writing assignments rhetorical. According to Campbell, by "incorporating a romantic belief in the organic nature of language, Buck hoped to make composition useful and vital to a changing student population" (xxxvi). Further, "Buck's rhetoric was more closely aligned with the Greek ideals of civic service than the mercantile and mechanical goals of current-traditional rhetoric" (xli).

In "The 'Advance' Toward Democratic Administration: Laura Johnson Wylie and Gertrude Buck of Vassar College" Suzanne Bordelon discusses the collaborative administration of these two women, Wylie as the chair of the department and Buck as the coordinator of rhetoric and Writing at Vassar College. Bordelon points out that Buck was profoundly influenced by John Dewey, who was at Michigan while she was a student, and argues that for Dewey and for Progressive Era educators like Wylie and Buck, education served a political function: to create a democratic society. The model of writing program administration that Buck developed with Wylie, based on Dewey's theories, emphasized the role of the faculty in the administrative process and made the department more inclusive and democratic. In the early years after its founding in 1861, Vassar, like many other colleges of the time, was organized around a family model: the president as well as the students lived on campus, and most of the faculty (and their families) lived in what was called the Main Building. But like other institutions, in the 1890s Vassar began to grow and organize itself into departmental units, and the administrative machinery became more sophisticated, with department chairs who were told explicitly that they were to be managers in the top-down manner that was being developed in the business world. Wylie viewed this managerial stage as necessary development toward a more democratic form of administration, in that it brought about a certain efficiency, but the need for a more inclusive model soon became obvious in a college whose faculty were active in social reform and the suffrage movement; faculty began to take more active roles in running the departments. Further, Wylie held an organic view of the department she chaired from 1897–1922; for her there were no separate (or inferior) branches but simply different aspects of or approaches to "English." Buck administered the writing and rhetoric program, and for her work was promoted to full professor and given a salary equal to that of the chair. Wylie's argument for this salary in her 1908–09 Report of the Department of English emphasizes the need in terms of the size of the department and subsequent administrative load:

> Of this administrative load, Miss Buck does her full share, relieving me entirely of a great deal of it. Indeed, if we did not work to-gether [*sic*] in entire harmony, it would be necessary either for me to do considerably less teaching, or to divide the department, as been unfortunately done in many places, into the departments of English or Rhetoric, and Lit-

> erature. The present union of the two subjects in a single department has many advantages of economy and efficiency, and it seems unfortunate that in order to preserve these, one of the people concerned should suffer serious and permanent financial loss. (qtd. in Bordelon 103–04)

JoAnn Campbell ("Women's Work, Worthy Work") points out that this cooperative administrative model was a product of the context in which it developed and the persons involved. The situation at Bryn Mawr about this same time demonstrates this fact in spades. In "'Replacing Nice Thin Bryn Mawr Miss Crandall with Fat, Harvard Savage': WPAs at Bryn Mawr College, 1902 to 1923," D'Ann George discusses the difficult relationship between Regina Crandall, the Director of the Essay Department, and the president of the university, who refused to grant her anything other than subordinate status in her administrative role. George documents how Crandall lobbied the president continually and unsuccessfully for faculty status, for more control over the curriculum, and for better working conditions for writing teachers. The president, M. Carey Thomas, had helped to found the college on the notion that gender stereotypes of women needed to be changed, and that women should share equal academic footing with men. But she did not see teaching writing or directing a writing program as legitimate academic work:

> Thomas couldn't legitimize Crandall's position because the male-dominated academic culture branded her work drudge work, unintellectual work, and therefore women's work. Thomas's way of battling gender stereotypes was not to challenge patriarchal value systems but to use Bryn Mawr to find a place for women—though not all women—in those systems. To value Crandall's work and position, in Thomas's eyes, would be to condemn all women to subordinate positions. (25)

Crandall and all the writing teachers received lower pay than the literature faculty, although if any writing teacher showed literary abilities he or she could be promoted to the literature faculty and never teach writing again; any faculty who showed an interest in continuing to teach writing were fired or replaced. The writing program was simply a vehicle for finding and eventually rewarding promising literature faculty. Crandall, having no authority over the curriculum or the hiring of faculty in the program she directed, fought back in a number of letters lobbying for better pay and working conditions for her faculty. Thomas asked her to resign and when she refused, Thomas replaced her with Howard Savage, a new graduate of Harvard with training in teaching English A there and with views of writing that were similar to those of Thomas. His salary was also that of a literature faculty member, and he taught literature as well as directing the writing program. Savage cut the program by reducing the number of required semesters of writing and by establishing an "efficient" method of grading papers (involving a set of symbols teachers could use), thus justifying an increase in class size to 80 students and a reduction in the number of teachers (from 7 to 4.5). Savage ultimately did not fare well at Vassar, leaving in 1923 for another position; as a writing program administrator he seems to have embodied James Sledd's caricature of the "boss compositionist," one who made the writing program efficient and cheap by making the curriculum formulaic and by hiring (women) faculty who worked for low pay and were content with a subordinate position, while he himself enjoyed full faculty status.

A number of historically Black colleges were also founded in the period just after the Civil War; the history of writing program administration at these institutions remains an area ripe for research. In "Sifting Through Fifty Years of Change: Writing Program Administration at an Historically Black Institution," Deany M. Cheramie discusses the difficulties of administration at Xavier University. Xavier was founded in 1915; in some ways it is atypical, since it is the only one of the 102 historically Black institutions that is also Catholic, but it is probably typical in other ways. Cheramie points out that like other such institutions, "Xavier was founded by a group of people who saw a need [. . .]. These people were dedicated to educating African Americans and giving them opportunities denied them by a lack of civil liberties. Yet the educators who had this calling quite often did not understand the needs of the students they were teaching" (146). The course descriptions reveal an effort on the part of the faculty to help their students fit a middle-class mold, which relied (and still relies) on a perceived standard associated with "white" middle class spoken and written English; students were expected to adapt their language to this standard, which resulted in numerous courses for "remediation" (147).

Archival evidence shows that although writing courses existed from the beginning of the university, the school was so poorly funded that administration in all areas was lean (usually carried out by the Sisters of the Blessed Sacrament who founded the institution), and was based in expediency—who could they afford to hire? Where could they fit the students? How many students could they get into a single class? (161). It was not until 50 years after its founding that Xavier was able to support a sufficient teaching staff, let alone a writing program administrator.

James Berlin, in *Rhetoric and Reality: Writing Instruction in American Colleges, 1900–1985,* gives some general background on writing programs during the period between World Wars I and II. He tells us that organized freshman composition programs led by directors became common in the 1920s and 1930s as enrollments in post-secondary education grew steadily. These programs, with various administrative procedures for dealing with students, were most common in the Midwestern and Western state institutions, but some also could be found at private universities such as Harvard and Bradley. "Their minimal essentials were a placement test, grouping students by ability, and some sort of procedure for verifying the success of the program, such as exit tests or follow-up programs for students who later displayed shortcomings" (65). He describes the program at Syracuse in the early twenties as typical. Its 1,200 freshman took a placement test that consisted of a writing selection and grammar questions, the tests were read by faculty to determine student placement into three categories: high, middle, and low. The highest group took only one course, English A, the middle group took English A and B, and the lowest group took English A, B, and C; English A was writing about literature. English B expository writing that included themes, a research paper, and a study of the correct forms of business and person correspondence. English C dealt with sentence structure, grammar, and spelling, focusing on correctness (66). There were attempts to ensure uniform grading standards via a model grading standard, a final exam for each course (a check on the performance of the teacher as well as of the students), and a requirement that teachers submit their final grades to a departmental committee on grading that had the authority to recommend changes (67). Berlin terms it a "technological model," one that emulated Harvard and was reflected in various forms at Illinois, Purdue, Wisconsin, Minnesota, UCLA, West Virginia, North Carolina State, and

Cornell (68). As Berlin points out, it was an attempt to provide for the needs of students with varying abilities, aiming at increasing chances for success for those who might otherwise fail; it was also—because of the fact that these courses were taught by graduate students and contingent faculty—an administrative model that involved above all surveillance and enforcement of curricula and standards. Betty Pytlik traces the development of TA training programs, which for the most part (up until the 1970s) involved such enforcement in "How Graduate Students Were Prepared to Teach Writing—1850–1970."

Although the persons who directed these programs were many and varied, the career of Stith Thompson gives us some insight into how composition, although not yet considered a scholarly discipline, could in fact help to advance a career path. Thompson had a long and distinguished career at Indiana University, where he directed and taught composition from 1921–37 as a young faculty member; his story is told in an essay by Jill Terry Rudy ("Building a Career by Directing Composition: Harvard, Professionalism, and Stith Thompson at Indiana University"). Rudy argues that although he later became known for his folklore scholarship, Thompson furthered his career trajectory with both composition and administration at a time when the notions of professionalism and disciplinary status systems were still emerging. With a PhD from Harvard, Thompson understood professional expectations about publication; his first publication, a composition textbook, was a foray into academic publishing that gave him name recognition and brought him the offer from Indiana, a step up the career ladder from his position at that time. Although this was from all accounts a leadership position within the department, Rudy points out that while it might help one gain a foothold in publishing, work in composition during the first half of the twentieth century was not a way to develop a scholarly reputation. After directing the program for a time, Thompson went on to become a folklore scholar. Rudy cautions against viewing this career trajectory as a bait and switch, since such a view assumes a disciplinary purity that was not extant. During his years as director he instituted placement tests, monitored grades, and generally "helped the Indiana composition program fulfill an important aim of professionalism: to train, sort, and credential future professionals" (83). Because there was not yet a scholarly tradition in the field, he could not reach the Distinguished Professorship at the top without publishing in literature, but composition helped him start to climb the career ladder successfully.

The Period of Professionalization: Post World War II

Like the Civil War before it, World War II and its aftermath brought enormous changes, not the least of which was a flood of enrollments in higher education; the Servicemen's Readjustment Act of 1944, known popularly as the G.I. Bill, had an enormous impact. One of the provisions of the Act was federal subsidies for attending colleges or other approved institutions; veterans were free to attend the college of their choice. Within the next 7 years, about 2,300,000 veterans took advantage of the educational benefits to attend colleges and universities (Butts and Cremin). Edward Corbett describes the situation in "A History of Writing Program Administration":

> English departments especially bore the brunt of that tidal wave of students because, in those days, virtually every college and university required all beginning students to take at least two years of English: a freshman English course and a sophomore survey course in either English or American literature. A veteran just beginning a college education became one of the twenty-five to thirty students who were packed into one of the dozens of newly created sections of freshman English. (65)

The professionalization of writing program administration began in large part because of this tidal wave, when English departments, especially those in public institutions, had to find some way of coordinating the ever-multiplying sections of freshman English. As Corbett characterizes the post-war period, it was a time of desperation in English departments; it didn't take long for departments to figure out that, with the escalating numbers, there would need to be a director or coordinator for such a huge course. Writing program administration was still a task rather than a position, but the seeds of professionalization were sown during this period as those in charge of such programs sought each other out for workable solutions to pressing problems such as staffing issues (where could one get enough qualified teachers to meet the demand for more sections?) and curriculum development (what was the best way to teach this new group of students?).

The most complete history to date of writing program administration during the period after World War II may be found in Amy Heckathorn's doctoral dissertation, "The Struggle Toward Professionalization: The Historical Evolution of Writing Program Administrators" (1999) and her subsequent essay, "Moving Toward a Group Identity: WPA Professionalism from the 1940s to the 1970s" (2004). Heckathorn outlines how early WPAs "began to come together to create a group identity, an evolution glimpsed through primary research in journals, books, and direct interviews which demonstrate that WPAs have struggled to transform themselves, and others' impressions of them, from bureaucratic managers of an undervalued discipline to dynamic administrators and theorists of their work and of their field" ("Moving" 191–92). She argues that although there were certainly writing program administrators before the Second World War, there was not yet a group identity. She points to the 1940s as the starting point for the formation of this professional group identity, dividing the period before the formation of the Council of Writing Program Administrators (1979) into what she terms the early era (1940–1963) and the transitional era (1964–1979); this latter category coinciding with what Robert Connors refers to as the "era of disciplinarity" in composition studies ("Composition History and Disciplinarity" 4). Heckathorn notes that these are in some sense artificial categories, but they provide a heuristic "for understanding how administrative work changed to meet the challenges of an evolving discipline" ("Moving" 192). Along with archival materials, interviews with experienced WPAs, and early publications, Heckathorn also gathered information from the MLA's *Job Information List* (begun in 1971); "in this discussion of employer needs . . . lie insights into the work and worth of the positions being advertised. WPAs' evolutionary changes are visible in these job descriptions—from early, undefined attempts to articulate the work of WPAs to later, more specific and complex descriptions of the roles WPAs would fill" (194).

Thomas Masters provides a general history of composition in the period just after World War II in *Practicing Writing: The Postwar Discourse of Freshman English*, based primarily on archival evidence from three institutions in Illinois (The University of Illinois in Urbana and what was then its branch campus in Chicago, Northwestern University, and Wheaton College). Masters found that the first priority at all three institutions was "the attempt to instill in students a code of correctness and style," that weekly papers were required in all three, and that the papers "were read not as attempts to convey or construct knowledge, but as proof that they had internalized the code" (136). Masters discusses the career of Charles Walter Roberts who was, like his counterparts at other large institutions who directed Freshman English, in charge of the legions of doctoral students who taught the course. The course, based on the sort of "mass production model" Brereton describes as common at large Midwestern universities after the turn of the twentieth century (*Origins* 470)

> exemplified the common sense, tightly managed, critically unselfconscious approach to the teaching of writing that many schools have emulated. In their "Memorial to Charles Walter Roberts," delivered after his death in 1968, his colleagues John Hamilton, Frank Moake, and Harris Wilson noted that "if one had been asked to name the most distinguished and influential director of the basic college writing course in the United States, one would have to name Charles Roberts[. . .]. Large numbers of Illinois PhDs who taught English composition under his direction . . . [have] become directors of composition and heads of departments in other colleges and universities throughout the United States." (Masters 9)

Roberts was in charge of a program that was squarely in the current-traditional mode, and he considered doing away with the elimination of Rhetoric 100 (the basic writing course of the time) as the apex of his career, since it placed responsibility for student literacy with the secondary schools (Masters 197). But he was also evidently an innovative and dedicated administrator, one of the co-founders of CCCC (he served as the organization's journal editor from 1950–1953). At Illinois he provided a day-by-day syllabus for his inexperienced teaching staff, began a publication entitled *The Green Cauldron* to publish exemplary student writing, and worked closely with the University Senate Committee on Student English to gather statistical data on student writing and publish handbooks for faculty (195). He also worked nationally as well as regionally to improve conditions for teachers and students (197).

Richard Lloyd-Jones gives some insight into what it was like to be a WPA at a large institution in the years after World War II, in a position like that of Roberts. Lloyd-Jones, himself (like Edward Corbett) a returning veteran, notes that it wasn't just a matter of numbers. War veterans were a different sort of student; "they were in a hurry, serious about learning, and not easily pushed aside" ("Doing as One Likes" 115). But faculty stepped up to the task. "One of the glories of our profession in the twentieth century is the legion of freshman directors who took over the onerous and often thankless job of planning a writing program, of setting up practicums to train the writing staff, of visiting the classes of callow teachers, and of fielding the complaints of parents and students" (Corbett "History" 67). Corbett notes that it is surprising how quickly these fearless individuals prepared themselves for the task and became resources for each other (and for their graduate TAs), given that there were no other resources at the time. Many of these newly minted administrators had literary backgrounds, but in some cases they had experience with teaching English in high school and with teacher training and supervision at the secondary level.[10]

The job of WPA was then, as now, often fraught with structural difficulties. After finishing his doctoral work, Richard Lloyd-Jones was appointed to run the technical writing program at Iowa, his qualifications being that he had taught in it. He details some of the issues in "Doing as One Likes." "Suddenly I was hiring teachers in a system that did not permit us to make appointments until after registration had confirmed enrollments, the day before classes began" (117). Like many of his counterparts in this era, Lloyd-Jones learned about writing program administration while doing it, adding courses to the program and transforming two existing graduate courses to focus on rhetorical theory and style. "No administrator ever enquired about what I was doing, so on my own I was creating a base for a program in non-fiction writing. That in turn meant that I had to be an autodidact, reading like mad to offer decent courses" (117). Like others in his situation, he became actively involved in NCTE, working on a committee that examined the state of knowledge about teaching composition; he notes modestly that the resulting publication, *Research in Written Composition*, was "well-received" (118). This book in fact marks the beginning of composition as an area of serious scholarship. In part because of his association with Richard Braddock, Lloyd-Jones soon found himself on the first NCTE Commission on Composition and the later on the CCCC Executive Committee, groups that he describes as "effectively two postdoctoral seminars" (118).

WPAs at this time often had free rein to develop programs. Like Lloyd-Jones, Theodore Baird was able to create a writing course at Amherst (a small, private men's institution) almost entirely single-handedly, a course that lasted from 1933 to 1966. Walker Gibson gives a general outline of the team-taught course in his essay on Baird; Gibson was himself one of the younger colleagues with whom Baird worked (in a "three years and out" instructorship [139]), a process that allowed elements of the course to be replicated elsewhere. In *Fencing with Words,* Robin Varnum shows how Baird became what we would now call a WPA, in large part because of the sheer strength of his personality as well as his vision of what a composition course should be and do.

Baird is best known for developing carefully sequenced writing assignments that required students to focus not on literature (as in many other institutions at the time) but on language and its uses. When asked about the purpose of the curriculum he developed and directed for some thirty years, Baird told Varnum: "We were interested in the way LANGUAGE makes order out of chaos. Over and over again we considered how language does this" (emphasis original 85). He described the course sequence, English 1–2, as a "laboratory course," noting that there are "no lectures, and the student does no required reading. Each student supplies his own subject matter for writing. That is, we ask the student to put into English what he has learned, both in and outside the classroom" (89). Baird worked with the five or six members of the department who taught the courses each year to develop a careful sequence of assignments; they met together once a week to debate and argue over the assignments, refining them as the years progressed. He set these meetings up in the hope that "by an exchange of ideas, by self-criticism, by argument, we can define our objects more clearly and use the best methods for achieving them that we know about" (5).

It was always clear that Baird was in charge, however. One colleague who worked with him in the 1960s as a young faculty intern described being mentored by Baird as "a terrifying experience" (205), and the course as an exercise in "liberal authoritarianism" (209). Students described English 1–2 as a sort of "boot camp," a very competitive male atmosphere (209) aimed at deliberately disorienting students (157, 161). Some found it quite stimulating, others were exasperated by it. As Varnum chronicles, the course was finally discontinued in the late 1960s, as new curricula were being developed as a response to the push for social change. Baird retired in 1970. He told Varnum he thought he had maintained English 1–2 as long as he had because "I scared them. They weren't quite brave enough to say, 'We are through with this.' If they [the English department] had said that, what could I have done? I had no authority, just my presence" (212); the course did, however, have a lasting influence on those who taught it. Many of these faculty took Baird's curricular ideas to their jobs at other institutions, where their presence still may be felt.[11]

THE FIRST PROFESSIONAL ORGANIZATION FOR WPAS: CCCC

Writing program administrators first began to organize after World War II, forming an organization called the Conference on College Composition and Communication; the first meeting was in 1949. Corbett notes that many of the prime movers of the new organization were from Big Ten schools in the Midwest; most of the workshops at the early meetings dealt with the administration of Freshman English ("A History" 68). There had, of course, been a few scattered meetings before then, organized for the mutual benefit of various groups of WPAs; Lisa Mastrangelo and Barbara L'Eplattenier document the meetings of the Intercollege Conference on English Composition organized by writing faculty from Mount Holyoke, Wellesley, Vassar, and Smith from 1919–1924, during the Progressive Era. But CCCC was the first attempt at a national organization, under the umbrella of an already-existing national organization, the National Council of Teachers of English.

The history of the early years of CCCC has been summarized by David Bartholomae in an essay that was his 1988 Chair's Address to the conference (published in 1989), "Freshman English, Composition, and CCCC." Drawing on pieces written by John Gerber and other early leaders in the organization, Bartholomae notes that it was an organization formed by those who needed to have discussions about practical concerns that existing venues like MLA and NCTE were not making possible (39). Richard Lloyd-Jones explains why those discussions were needed: "The folks who came to that meeting were pressed by what seemed to be a crisis and wanted to have practical talk about how to deal with a flood of new students—many of whom were first-generation college students, most somewhat older veterans [. . .]. In a single year—1946—college enrollments had doubled" ("Who We Were, Who We Should Become" 487). The fact that their colleagues did not understand the work that they were doing was also a reason for these newly appointed WPAs to band together. John Gerber, the first Chair of CCCC, in a 1975 paper entitled "Loomings" (evoking the first chapter of *Moby Dick*) recalled the angst of those who had taken over the new quasi-administrative position of director of freshman English and who organized the meeting:

> We were [like Ishmael] indeed grim about the mouth [. . .]. We believed that we had devised new methods of instruction, better ways of evaluation, and more reliable ways of reading student papers. We worked harder, we were sure, than our colleagues. Nevertheless, despite all this and more, we remained second-class citizens. Department chairmen thinly praised us each fall and then forgot about us for the rest of the year. Eighteenth-century scholars looked down their noses at us and medievalists barely tolerated us. So we decided to go to sea—that is, to organize. (2)

Some of the very first workshops (held in Chicago in 1950 and published in the May 1950 *CCC*) give the flavor of this new professional organization: "The Function of the Composition Course in General Education," "Objectives and Organization of the Composition Course," "The Organization and Use of the Writing Laboratory," "Freshman English for Engineers," and "Administration of the Composition Course." This latter workshop was repeated at several consecutive meetings (a precursor of the Council of Writing Program Administrators' Workshops begun in 1982).

In the early years, CCCC was a relatively small organization; Edward Corbett notes that even in the early 1970s when he was Program Chair for the convention in Seattle, he felt lucky if they could attract 300 people ("How I Became a Teacher of Composition" 5). Its focus was practical; the early meetings were workshops focused on the most pressing common problems directors were facing, and the journal that developed out of the meetings was at first a venue for reporting on those workshops and discussing what many contributors referred to as the "problem" of freshman English. Many experimental approaches were in the air as a result of the communications movement, in part an outgrowth of training programs that had sprung up during the war to get GIs up to speed for wartime tasks in what was in many ways the country's first technological war; David Russell discusses this movement at some length in *Writing in the Academic Disciplines*.

> The massive postwar influx of GIs into higher education made colleges and universities receptive to the idea of a communications course, for it combined scientific and patriotic rationales with managerial efficiency. Enrollment tripled between 1945 and 1949, sparking a host of experiments with communications courses. But unlike the military programs, which integrated writing instruction into technical courses, these were essentially core courses, which combined speech and composition, sometimes adding elements of the new field of semantics, particularly the analysis of propaganda and advertising. (259)

Composition and Communication eventually went their separate ways as disciplines, as detailed by Diana George and John Trimbur (in "The 'Communication Battle,' or Whatever Happened to the 4th C?" and by John Heyda in "Fighting Over Freshman English: CCCC's Early Years and the Turf Wars of the 1950s"). But evidence from the early years of the journal shows that much of a freshman English director's time was taken up not only with administrative issues but also with designing entirely new curricula to meet the needs of a new group of students, in part in discussions with colleagues from communication but also with those in the emerging discipline of linguistics.

Several articles and workshop reports from the early years of CCCC document administrative efforts to deal with the crush of students. For example, in "Freshman English During the Flood" (1956), Charlton Laird describes a timesaving plan to help teachers deal with the influx of students: peer tutoring. Rather than meeting three times a week as a class, the students met only once, spending the rest of the time in groups, reading and commenting upon each others' papers. There is, however, little evidence of a research base for any of the early articles in *CCC,* let alone those that specifically focus on writing program administration as a field for study. The lone exception is an article entitled "Administration of the Freshman English Program" (1955) in which Emerson Shuck reported the results of a survey he conducted to study current practice, listing common concerns that emerged from his study: class size, teaching load, type of course, student placement, remedial programs, establishing proficiency in composition, the administrative structure of the program, and administrative tasks. In "Loomings" (1975) John Gerber noted the deficiencies of those early CCCC conversations and publications:

> We rarely talked about teaching as a process. Had we done so we would have been more concerned about the nature of those at the receiving end, namely the students. I find almost nothing in the programs or in the *Bulletin* [*CCC*] about the particular nature of the students in the fifties, and the need for adapting our teaching such persons. What is surprising about this is that the students of the fifties, especially of the early fifties, were a very special breed [. . .]. It was the period of the Korean War, and of Senator Joseph McCarthy and his hunt for commies and perverts. In some ways it was as sick a period as we have ever been through. Even liberal Americans had lost their sense of humor and were downright frightened, many of them, that they would be singled out by McCarthy and his henchmen. No wonder that *Time* magazine in 1951 called college students grave, conventional, apathetic, and fatalistic. A Purdue poll showed that the majority of them had little confidence in the freedom assured by the Bill of Rights. In 1953 Thornton Wilder used the term that has been applied to them ever since: they were, he wrote in the *Yale Daily News,* the "silent generation." (11)

Gerber closes by referring to Emerson's concept of the scholar in his right state as "man thinking," and in his degenerate state, when the victim of society, a mere thinker, or worse, a parrot of other's thinking. Gerber declares that "if we had any basic weakness in the 1950's it was that we were sentences and paragraphs and not men and women thinking" (12). Dwight Purdy, in "A Polemical History of Freshman Composition in Our Time," opines that in spite of the fact that there were some dedicated directors, much WPA work was haphazard and poorly done during this period, when most directors were amateurs.

> An assistant professor took on the odious job of directing freshman English for tenure's sake. He (always he then) had some interest in teaching composition but none in constructing and managing a durable program, and the only theory he knew was Aristotle. I exaggerate a bit. There were dedicated directors about. I knew some. But the untenured assistant professor coerced by senior professors was more common. From this estranged figure came mismanagement, or none at all. The twenty, forty, or four hundred teaching assistants in his care were often selected by no rational principle. None of their course work had a thing to do with composition [. . .]. The director chose common texts with little or no consultation and more than likely set up a program without a coherent structure
>
> [. . .] He was overwhelmed. (793)

The Birth of the Council of Writing Program Administrators

As Neal Lerner points out, the two greatest influxes of students into higher education occurred during the years 1879–1880, when there was a 122 percent increase in enrollments, and the baby boom year 1969–1970, when there was a 120 percent increase (188). The 1960s and 1970s were revolutionary decades in academe for more reasons than sheer numbers, including, among other changes, the paradigm shift in composition studies from a current-traditional focus on the finished product to a focus on students' writing processes; Donald Murray's "Teach Writing as Process Not Product" (1972) became a rallying cry for WPAs who were involved in staff development and/or TA training programs. This period also marks the beginning of composition as a discipline in its own right. A number of markers may be used to demonstrate this fact. Most often quoted is the 1963 publication of *Research in Written Composition* (Braddock et al.), which was both a summary of research so far and a call for a research agenda in the field. At the same time, the Commission on English of the College Entrance Examination Board was holding a series of institutes to improve the academic preparation and pedagogy of English teachers in the schools, a format followed by subsequent institutes for teachers established by the National Defense Education Act in 1964; Richard Lloyd-Jones documents these institutes and also the rise of the National Writing Project in "On Institutes and Projects." (Lloyd-Jones notes that in 1979 and 1980, NEH funded two six-month institutes for College Directors of Freshman Composition. Some of the materials developed in those workshops later appeared in *Courses for Change,* edited by Carl Klaus and Nancy Jones, a collection with an emphasis on program reform [163–64]). These institutes, Lloyd-Jones argues, helped to establish composition as scholarly and professional work at the university level. One can also point to the rise of professional journals in the field, as documented by Maureen Goggin (*Authoring a Discipline: Scholarly Journals and the Post-World War II Emergence of Rhetoric and Composition*), the increasing numbers of doctoral programs emphasizing rhetoric and composition (as documented in periodic surveys in *Rhetoric Review*), and in the case of WPAs, the increasingly sophisticated job descriptions appearing in the MLA's *Job Information List* (as documented in Heckathorn's dissertation). Specialized professional organizations, often off-shoots of the larger ones, were beginning to form as well among people with common concerns and issues, not all of them having to do with research and teaching; the Associations of Departments of English, an organization for English department chairs, was formed in 1962, and The Council of Writing Program Administrators was born in the late 1970s.

The period was one of social ferment. The Civil Rights Movement, the Women's Movement (growing out of the Civil Rights Movement), and the Anti-War Movement were all factors that contributed to social unrest and discussions of needed changes in university curricula. After a dip in college enrollments in the late 1950s (when the WWII veterans finished their education), there was an upsurge of enrollments as baby boomers began to enroll in ever-increasing numbers. At the same time, graduate programs were expanding at research institutions; as

Carol Hartzog documents in *Composition and the Academy,* freshman composition became a means to support graduate students in English departments, which led to an increased need for TA training. Community colleges, which had existed in small numbers since the turn of the century, became the new growth industry in higher education, in part to deal with the sheer numbers of students but also in part because of the growing democratization of higher education, a sense that everyone, not just the elite few, had a right to attend college. Affirmative Action legislation and Educational Opportunity Programs helped to ensure that those who had previously been denied access to higher and graduate education would now be included. In the 1960s, 457 new community colleges opened their doors, and the American Association of Community Colleges was formed during that same decade. (Today, according to the website for the Association, community colleges educate more than half of college graduates in the nation.) Responding to this growth, NCTE and CCCC began in 1965 to support the development of two-year college regional conferences, an arrangement that eventually resulted in the formation of the Two-Year College English Association.

In his history of writing in the academic disciplines, David Russell discusses the institutional responses to the influx of students from an increasingly diverse group of students, many of them first-generation college students.

> Like [racial] integration, the rapid growth in numbers forced colleges to face the task of initiating students whose language background was radically different. For example, one of those new institutions, City University of New York (CUNY), began project SEEK [a program for students from low income areas of the city, which meant its population was mostly African American and Hispanic] in 1965 to prepare students whose grades excluded them from admission. Social and political upheavals in the late 1960s forced CUNY to begin open admissions in 1970, five years earlier than planned. Out of that experience, Mina Shaughnessy, a former copy editor and part-time writing instructor at CUNY, founded the study of *basic writing* [. . .]. (274–75)

A group of faculty interested in and dedicated to this newly-named field of basic writing began to meet regularly on Saturdays at the Graduate Center to talk to each other and help each other out as they explored ways of helping this new group of students. These faculty included Mina Shaughnessy and her group at City College, Kenneth Bruffee at Brooklyn College, Sondra Perl at Hostos Community College, Harvey Wiener at LaGuardia, Bob Lyons and Don McQuade at Queens, and Charles Bazerman at Baruch College (Bazerman, "Looking" 22; Wiener interview and e-mail; Brereton "Symposium"). Harvey Wiener organized the group into a more formal body, the CUNY Association of Writing Supervisors (CAWS); this was an organization that provided some of the structure and much of the leadership for the nationwide organization about to be born.

During this period the Modern Language Association was restructuring itself, responding to what amounted to a revolt among some of its members who demanded a more democratically run organization (as detailed by Richard Ohmann in *English in America: A Radical View of the Profession* 34–5). The various committees that controlled the program were restructured into divisions in 1975, including a new Division on the Teaching of Writing, sponsoring their first sessions at the December 1976 meeting (Papp). MLA required a planning committee to organize the sessions; Ken Bruffee recalls that the committee consisted of Edward Corbett, Winifred Bryan Horner, Harvey Wiener, and himself (e-mail). They organized a number of sessions[12] successfully and then pressed for one more; it was Wiener's idea to use that meeting to form a national organization for writing program directors. That session, described on p. 1054 of the 1976 program as an "organization meeting for a writing program administrators' council," was scheduled for the last day of the conference, at 11:00 a.m.; Bruffee recalls that MLA, "typically skeptical of our importance," assigned the group a closet-size room (e-mail). What the organizers themselves had visualized as a fairly small group of people who wanted to learn from each other (and then adjourn to cry in their beer, according to Winifred Bryan Horner ["WPA Presidents' Forum"]), turned out to be a packed session, full of directors of writing programs from across the country. Those who attended, Horner among them, remember that the atmosphere was electric. The notion of a national organization was brought up. Harvey Wiener was immediately nominated as president, Horner as vice president, and Elaine Maimon was included in the newly elected board as a representative from small liberal arts colleges. The name of the new organization was chosen deliberately, its initials (WPA) a nod to the New Deal (Wiener interview).

Because the machinery of CAWS was already up and running, the new organization—in effect, CAWS gone national—was formed in just a few months. The constitution and by-laws were approved in early 1977; among the goals articulated were "to serve the interests of writing programs by educating the academic community and the public at large about the needs of successful writing programs" and "to promote cooperation among the various writing programs in [. . .] colleges throughout the country by sharing information and by defining common interests and needs" (Council "Bylaws" 61). The organization issued its first publication in March of that year, *WPA: A Newsletter for Writing Program Administration*, edited and distributed by Robert Farrell (who was running the writing program at Cornell). It consisted of a statement of purpose for the organization, a draft form for a national handbook on writing programs, a list of WPAs with addresses and a list broken down by type of institution, and an editorial comment. The newsletter became a referred journal, *WPA: Writing Program Administration,* in 1979, bound in a distinctive red cover (chosen—again deliberately—by its first editor, Bruffee, to suggest the subversive nature of WPA work).[13] The journal, back issues of which are now online and available from the Council of Writing Program Administrators website, contains essays on every aspect of a WPA's work.

The organization was fortunate not only in being able to build on an already existing structure, but also in its first president. Harvey Wiener got the organization noticed immediately; he identified sessions at both MLA and CCCC, and organized panels for those meetings. Together with the WPA Executive Committee, which began meeting for an entire day at CCCC, he set up workshops for new WPAs so that they could learn from their more experienced counterparts; the first of these was held at Martha's Vineyard, August 7–15, 1982, and was reported on by one of the participants in the Spring 1983 issue of the journal (Zelnick). Wiener himself and Tim Donovan of Northeastern University ran the workshop as part of Northeastern's summer program. As the first of its kind, it was an experiment, evidently a not altogether successful one. In an analysis of the workshop evaluations published in the WPA journal, Zelnick (who had attended the workshop) noted that the attendees complained that the organizers "refused to specify a few set issues" but had instead decided on a "loosely organized process of discovery" (11). The small problem-solving group sessions were also a source of frustration, since participants came from such different institutions and had such varying levels of experience that they had no common ground. But Zelnick also opined that the workshop was valuable in that it helped form a network of colleagues, a more secure identity as a professional, and an awareness of the organization and its resources (14). The workshop has continued—to much more enthusiastic evaluations—up to the present day, adding an annual conference in 1986; the conference was reported on by Lynn Bloom and Richard Gebhardt in the Spring 1987 *WPA: Writing Program Administration*, offering advice to future conference and workshop organizers. Wiener also worked to get the organization affiliated with other national organizations, including CCCC (which did not take long) and MLA (which did).

Wiener went after grant monies for the fledgling organization. The Exxon Foundation gave WPA three start-up grants to establish the Consultant-Evaluator Program (and to help pay the evaluators), and then endowed the program with a larger grant. (At the time he wrote the grants, Wiener was an evaluator for the Middle States Association of Colleges and Schools; he wrote the proposals based in part on that experience.) The Consultant-Evaluator Program provided—and continues to provide—outside evaluators to give expert advice on the organization and administration of writing programs, which are sometimes neglected in the regular evaluations of departments of English. The organization printed the guidelines for the evaluation of writing programs in the journal, thus providing campuses that could not afford a campus visit with some notion of what a program assessment should look like (Wiener interview). More recently, the organization has established a fund for research to which WPAs can apply.

But perhaps the most important thing that the new organization did was to coin the term that described the work: writing program administrator. Harvey Wiener believes that this was a major contribution to the profession, adding "a dignifying occupational tag to the parlance" which "bestowed a new level of legitimacy" to the job (2000). Just after World War II, when the rapid growth of universities demanded more formal administrative structures, various existing members of the English Department were asked to take on the task of administration, but were called "freshman composition coordinators" or "directors of composition." As Richard Bullock states, it was "a shared burden rotated, as are many chairmanships, among all faculty" (14); medievalists, specialists in nineteenth century romantic literature, Shakespeareans, Melville scholars, or the faculty members who taught the secondary education methods classes were put in charge of designing a curriculum and training the rapidly growing numbers of teaching assistants. Writing in 1958, John P. Noonan noted that these faculty were chosen on the basis of their administrative ability and personality rather than any particular special background or training they might possess. It was not considered a professional task, but was considered university service.

Although this system was based on the notion that anyone trained in English literature knew enough about composition to be able to run a writing program, it did have the virtue of putting people with at least some seniority and knowledge of the university in charge of the administrative tasks required, and it occurred during a time when service to the department was a more important part of tenure decisions (as noted by Purdy, an assistant professor could take on the job "for tenure's sake" 793). This situation changed as composition became a discipline in its own right—when, as Stephen North puts it, composition became Composition (15). As doctoral programs in composition and rhetoric developed in the late 1970s and 1980s, English departments began to hire the graduates of these programs to take over (as documented by Chapman and Tate in 1987). Wendy Bishop, herself one of these graduates at the time, wrote one of the earliest pieces attempting to define the role that these new disciplinary specialists were expected to take on, "Toward a Definition of a Writing Program Administrator: Expanding Roles and Evolving Responsibilities." In this piece she includes many of the administrative duties that were being assigned to these young faculty: student placement and record keeping, course staffing, program accountability, and curriculum development. Bishop's piece was a signal to neophytes as to what they could expect in their new roles as newly named WPAs.

Problems developed immediately for these young instant administrators. Although having someone with a disciplinary specialty in composition in charge of writing programs made eminent sense, having a brand new assistant professor in an administrative role did not. As Patricia Bizzell says in her foreword to Diana George's collection,

Kitchen Cooks, Plate Twirlers and Troubadours: Writing Program Administrators Tell Their Stories, a WPA

> may teach and do research in his or her area of graduate training, but this work consists of only a small fraction of the job. The administrator must consider issues of budget, curricular planning, personnel management, technological support, physical plant—a veritable host of issues—and must deal with a wide range of people, from students to professional subordinates and peers to power brokers in academic high places, to address these issues. Graduate training [. . .] does not—and perhaps cannot possibly—prepare a person for these demands." (viii)

As the essays in George's collection show in often painful detail, many of these new hires were completely unprepared for such a position; their doctoral programs had not included any study of or experience with administration, they did not have the lived experience that would help with administrative decision-making, and their junior status meant that they had difficulty taking on the leadership role an administrator needs to assume. (The title of Keith Rhodes's essay gives the flavor of the stories told in this book: "Mothers, Tell Your Children Not to Do What I have Done: The Sin and Misery of Entering the Profession as a Composition Coordinator.")

To compound the problem, this period of time was also one in which universities across the country were ramping up their tenure and promotion expectations to coincide with those of the most elite research institutions: publish or perish. During the 1980s the position of writing program administrator became a revolving door at many institutions; new PhDs were hired to do administration and then told at the end of six years that their work counted only as service, and that they had not published enough to get tenure. The tale of tenure denied became so common that in 1989 the Conference on College Composition and Communication, in its Statement of Principles and Standards, called for having the WPA position held only by tenured faculty; an article written by Gary Olson and Joseph Moxley at about the same time (and cited frequently thereafter) endorsed the same system. Wendy Bishop and Gay Lynn Crossley document the difficulties that arose in "Doing the Hokey Pokey? Why Writing Program

Administrators' Job Conditions Don't Seem to Be Improving." The main problem was that, now that there was a disciplinary specialist in composition, English departments felt justified in assigning that person everything having to do with writing; the job definitions being generated as a result were so complex that no one person could possibly manage the position (47).

The response was a series of exhortations from scholars in the field and position statements issued by the Council of Writing Program Administrators. In 1987 Richard Bullock called for viewing WPAs not as "caretakers of a slice of bureaucracy" but as administrators who were also "experts and scholars testing and refining their knowledge in the practical area of application" (14). In an oft-quoted essay entitled "Use It or Lose It: Power and the WPA," Edward M. White argues that seizing and using power is an essential part of the WPA's role, exhorting WPAs not to accept conditions of powerlessness but to empower themselves through "good arguments, good data, and good allies, mixed with caution and cunning" (7). (The military metaphors White uses suggest the feelings of embattlement at the time: "In order to assess our situations, we need to assess where the enemies of our program lurk, what their motives and weapons are, and how we can marshal forces to combat them" [6].) Although the revolving door for new WPAs is still far from rare, the situation began to change in the last decade of the twentieth century.

The 1990 WPA summer conference (the same conference at which James Sledd coined the term "boss compositionist") was organized around the theme of "Status, Standards, and Quality." At that meeting members of the workshop that preceded the conference discussed the issue of status and the intellectual work of the WPA; some of them began to formulate a resolution. Christine Hult, then editor of *WPA: Writing Program Administration,* presented a paper at the conference about the conflicted status of writing program administrators and invited those present to "begin a dialogue toward formulation of a statement of professional standards by the WPA organization. Such a statement would outline prerequisites for effective administration of writing programs as well as equitable treatment of WPAs" (Hult et al., 88). The conversations that started in the workshop and continued during the conference eventuated in a draft document drawn up by the end of the conference known as "The Portland Resolution."[14] A committee was set up by the Council of Writing Program Administrators to review and revise the draft; it was accepted by the Executive Committee and published by Hult and her committee in 1992. The document outlines the untenable job situations for many WPAs at that time (unrealistic expectations, little recognition for their work, few resources) and presents guidelines for the effective administration of writing programs: writing clear job descriptions, setting forth clear guidelines for the evaluation of WPAs, establishing job security and stability for them, ensuring access to the individuals and units that influence their programs, and making sure that they have the resources and budget to run quality programs. Not long after, the Council developed a second position statement, "Evaluating the Intellectual Work of Writing Program Administration"; this document, discussed in detail earlier (in Chapter 2), was intended to set out guidelines for tenure and promotion evaluations, but has also served as an official statement about the nature of the WPA's work as intellectual as well as managerial. It has also served as a useful guideline for outside evaluators writing letters for the tenure and promotion of writing program administrators.

The Development of *WPA: Writing Program Administration*

In "Professionalizing Politics," Richard Ohmann writes:

> A group of workers turns itself into a profession by grounding its practice in a body of knowledge, developing and guarding that knowledge within a universally recognized institution such as a university; limiting access to its lore and skills by requiring aspirants to pass through graduate or professional programs; and controlling the certification of those aspirants for practice either by widespread agreement among employers (for example, to hire only those philosophers or biologists who have earned doctoral degrees) or with the backing and enforcement of the State (as in medicine, law, public school teaching, and so on). (227)

The journal of the Council of Writing Program Administrators, more than any other scholarly journal in the rapidly developing field of composition and rhetoric, provided a venue for the growing body of knowledge about writing program administration during the 1980s and 1990s, helping it become a recognized sub-field of composition and rhetoric. In a 1985 article that reviewed the years of his editorship, Bruffee commented that the articles fell into three categories: how-to articles, contextual how-to articles, and professional identity articles (6). Ten years later, Christine Hult, editor from 1988 to 1994, traced the professionalization of the journal in "The Scholarship of Administration." Bruffee had observed that up to 1985, most articles were of the first type, a few of the second, and very few of the third; Hult observed that by the end of her term as editor, the balance had shifted considerably toward the second and third as WPAs strove towards a professional identity (125). Hult pointed out that the journal gradually came to exemplify what Ernest Boyer termed the "scholarship of administration," which she defined as "the systematic, theory-based production of a dynamic program (as opposed to traditional scholarship which is generally defined as the production of 'texts'). Because it is dynamic, it more nearly resembles the productions of our colleagues in music, theater, or dance, but demands no less 'scholarly' expertise than that required by the performance of a Bach cantata" (126–27). She called for the establishment of departmental and university guidelines for tenure and promotion that include this sort of scholarship for WPAs.

As noted earlier, the Council of Writing Program Administrators developed and published documents that have further aided the professionalization of the field: the Portland Resolution, which outlined the work that a WPA could be expected to do, and a position statement, "Evaluating the Intellectual Work of Writing Program Administration." These documents, backed by Boyer's work in redefining the nature of "scholarship," have helped to raise the professional status of the WPA in an institutional sense.

Writing Program Administration in the Twenty-First Century

In 2001 the Council of Writing Program Administrators sponsored a conference entitled "Composition Studies in the 21st Century"; out of that conference came *Composition Studies in the New Millennium: Rereading the Past, Rewriting the Future*, edited by the conference organizers, Lynn Z. Bloom, Donald A. Daiker, and Edward M. White. It is interesting to compare the topics in this volume with those in the early issues of *CCC* and of *WPA: Writing Program Administration*. Where the journal articles were for the most part discussions of very practical, hands-on issues of the "how to" variety (as Bruffee described them), the sections of this book focus on macro-issues. It is organized around a series of questions: "What Do We Mean by Composition Studies—Past, Present, and Future?", "What Do/Should We Teach When We Teach Composition?", "Where Will Composition be Taught and Who Will Teach It?", "What Theories, Philosophies Will Undergird Our Research Paradigms? And What Will Those Paradigms Be?", "How Will New Technologies Change Composition Studies?", "What Languages Will Our Students Write and What Will They Write About?", and "What Political and Social Issues Have Shaped Composition Studies in the Past and Will Shape This Field in the Future?" Each question has two essays devoted to it by a noted scholar in the field and a response from a third; most of the contributors were, at least at one point in their careers, writing program administrators.

The Council of Writing Program Administrators has grown from a small, local organization to a national one, boasting a newsletter, a refereed journal, an annual workshop and conference, a research grant program, and has current affiliations with the Association of American Colleges, MLA, CCCC, and NCTE. In 1991 David Schwalm started the WPA listserv, a list that has served to put WPAs in touch with one another electronically, providing a venue for an invisible college of WPAs across the nation. Today this listserv is sometimes the first introduction a new WPA has to writing program administration as a profession. But one of the more interesting developments in the profession is the fact that the position of WPA has become the training ground for university administration in general; Elaine Maimon, now Chancellor of the University of Alaska, Anchorage, has said at many meetings that everything she ever learned about being a college administrator she learned as a WPA. Many former WPAs are now serving as department chairs, deans, and upper-level administrators. David Schwalm (himself a Vice Provost) discusses some of the reasons for this in "Writing Program Administration as Preparation for an Administrative Career": "Being a WPA taught me about the need to see issues in a larger context, to take broader views, to accept less than 100 percent solutions, to recognize that although there is a season for deliberation, there is also a season for decisiveness" (133). Writing program administration has become, for many, part of a career path in higher education administration.

4 Current Issues and Practical Guidelines

There are several books that give overviews of current issues as well as practical advice for WPAs. Although they were published in the 1980s, Edward White's *Developing Successful College Writing Programs* and Tomas Hilgers and Joy Marsella's *Making Your Writing Program Work* both have material that is still useful. More recently (2002), *The Writing Program Administrator's Resource: A Guide to Reflective Institutional Practice,* edited by Stuart Brown and Theresa Enos, provides essays by experienced WPAs on a range of topics, and includes an annotated bibliography on issues in writing program administration (Jackson and Wojahn). This book also has appendices that include the "Portland Resolution," the position statement from the Council of Writing Program Administrators on "Evaluating the Intellectual work of WPAs," and the "WPA Outcomes Statement for First-Year Composition." The *Allyn & Bacon Sourcebook for Writing Program Administrators,* edited by Irene Ward and William Carpenter, likewise has essays from experienced WPAs, and includes even more primary references in the appendices: the "CCCC Statement of Principles and Standards for the Postsecondary Teaching of Writing," the "Portland Resolution," the "WPA Outcomes Statement for First-Year Composition," the "Guidelines for the Workload of the College English Teacher" (from the NCTE College Section Steering Committee), the "CCCC Position Statement on the Preparation and Professional Development of Teachers of Writing," the "WPA Statement on Evaluating the Intellectual Work of the WPA," the Association of Departments of English "Guidelines for Class Size and Workload for College and University Teachers of English," the Buckley Amendment (the Family Educational Rights and Privacy Act of 1974), and the "Guidelines for Self-Study to Precede a WPA Consultant-Evaluators Visit." Linda Myers-Breslin's *Administrative Problem-Solving for*

Writing Programs and Writing Centers: Scenarios in Effective Program Management, provides case studies having to do with selection and training of staff and TAs, program development, and various professional issues, all written by experienced WPAs. In what follows, I will deal with resources specifically focusing on curriculum, pedagogy, assessment and accountability, staffing and staff development, and administrative and professional issues for WPAs.

Curriculum

First-Year Composition

The term *curriculum* can refer to a series of courses and also to the content of those courses. Most universities have at least one introductory writing course already in place, often "first-year composition" or "freshman composition." Many also require a prior course in developmental or basic writing, and a subsequent lower-division course—an artifact of the time when English departments designed the first course to focus on "expository prose" and the second on "writing about literature." Now, however, the subsequent course sometimes focuses on research, sometimes on argument, sometimes on other issues; sometimes there is a third course called "advanced composition" in the upper-division which often focuses on professional/technical writing. Further, the introductory course and sometimes a second writing course are almost always part of the general education program, meaning that the WPA in charge of the program is responsible not only to his or her department but to the institution at large. First-year writing courses are often part of what has become known as the "First Year Experience," facilitating the transition from high school to college; the National Resource Center for the First Year Experience and Students in Transition (housed at the University of South Carolina) holds conferences and seminars and publishes materials, some of which are relevant to curriculum development. Edward White's book *Developing Successful College Writing Programs* devotes an entire chapter to the issue of the place of writing within the undergraduate curriculum, advising that one needs to

> follow just a few commonsense guidelines that follow from conceiving the writing class as a critical thinking course fundamental to the liberal arts curriculum

[: . .]: focus on writing in the class, maintain an appropriate intellectual content, plan for discovery and revision, organize a series of writing tasks that relate to each other and call for a broad range of writing and reading skills. (67)

Unlike introductory mathematics or chemistry, there is no set body of knowledge that writing courses have to convey; writing courses are more like studio art or acting classes in that they focus on guided practice of a particular skill. What, then, should students be reading and writing about? The entries under the heading "Curriculum Development" in *The Bedford Bibliography for Teachers of Writing* (Reynolds, Bizzell, and Herzberg) are so varied and eclectic as to be bewildering to a novice WPA. In "Composition at the Turn of the Twenty-First Century," Richard Fulkerson attempts to make sense of the variety of approaches by trying to decide, based on scholarly publications and textbooks, what is actually going on in classrooms. Fulkerson traces various trends, including the growth of what he calls cultural/critical studies, the "quiet expansion of expressive approaches," and the split of rhetorical approaches into three areas: argumentation, genre analysis, and preparation for the academic discourse community (654). Fulkerson concludes that the major divide in approaches " is no longer expressive personal writing versus writing for readers [. . .] . The major divide is instead between a postmodern, cultural studies, reading-based program, and a broadly conceived rhetoric of genres and discourse forums" (679). He notes that determining whether the cultural studies approach "is as widespread in composition classrooms as in our journals is actually an open question" that would require survey data we do not have (659). We will in fact have such data soon, from a project being run by Kathleen Blake Yancey and some of her former colleagues at Clemson University ("Portraits"). Data from more than 1850 respondents indicates that the overwhelming majority of these had curricula that focused on introducing students to the discourse of academic writing.[1]

David Smit has attempted to trace the development of curricula in writing courses over time. In "Curriculum Design for First-Year Writing Programs" he describes the "current-traditional" approach that was inherited from the nineteenth century, the "burst of creativity in discourse theory" of the 1970s (in the work of Kinneavy, Britton and Moffett) and the accompanying rise of the process approach, and the "social turn" of the late 1980s and 1990s that emphasized the contextual nature of meaning and the way writing varies according to that context (186–87). As a result of the social turn, most current theories of writing are now what Nystrand and his colleagues call functional, constructivist, contextual, and dialogic (301–12). Smit states that these four theories have produced four new frameworks for designing first-year composition: cultural studies and critical pedagogy, introduction to discourse, ethnographic, and service learning (195), all of which he discusses in detail. He concludes by listing some things WPAs need to consider when deciding on a particular curriculum, including theoretical issues (What is writing? How is writing learned? Is there a single writing process, or are there many different writing processes? What basic form of instruction should be used? How should writing in a course be evaluated?), and the practical implications of those issues (What background and experience in teaching writing have your instructors and graduate teaching assistants had? Should you have materials in common? What background and experience have your students had? What will the other stakeholders in first-year writing think about your new curriculum? Should first-year writing courses be required of all first-year students or only of those who "need" them? What resources have you been given to develop a new curriculum? Should you use available textbooks or develop your own materials?) (200–03).

In *Making Your Writing Program Work: A Guide to Good Practices,* Hilgers and Marsella provide advice about building a curriculum for a writing program. They point out that politics have a powerful role in disputes over writing pedagogy; WPAs are always dealing with constituencies that identify writing instruction with remediation, forms and formats, and correct usage, a view that most WPAs find reductive. As they state, "What is taught, how it is taught, and why it is taught are all inextricably intertwined" in a writing curriculum (27). Further, every curriculum is embedded in a particular site and context; an appropriate curriculum for one school and group of students may not be appropriate for another. Any curriculum must be guided by research and theories of learning and composing, have a philosophical coherence, and include good practices that are consistent with both theory and philosophy. Hilgers and Marsella lay out some questions for WPAs to ask as they think about curriculum construction: questions about philosophical beliefs and values, about theories of learning and writing, and about practices. Among these are:

- Can the program's teachers work comfortably with the [program's] philosophy?
- Is the curriculum's view of learners consonant with how the program's learners act?
- Are the goals of the curriculum's philosophy related to the real goals of students, teachers, and administrators?
- Does the curriculum create real contexts for real learning?
- Are classroom teachers involved in every aspect of the curriculum, from construction through evaluation?
- Does the curriculum use writing in many different contexts in many different forms?
- Does the curriculum use writing for many different purposes?
- Does the curriculum make clear why the writing is being done—how it fits into the bigger picture?
- Does the curriculum place written texts in language-rich environments, and foster interactions involving students' texts?
- Does the curriculum provide varied resources to help students to improve different types of writing?
- Does the curriculum provide different forms of reader response to student texts, at appropriate points in the writing process?
- Do writing activities convey positive attitudes toward student writers and build on the diverse kinds of knowledge they bring to their classrooms?
- Do writing assignments encourage engagement and real thinking?
- Are course textbooks congruent with the values, theoretical positions, and practices [of learning theory and research]?
- Does the curriculum provide room for teachers to explore, adapt, and evaluate—in other words, to act as researchers in trying to improve instruction and student writing?

- Does the overall school environment allow good curricular practices to take hold?
- Does the curriculum reward good writing? (30–46)

Perhaps the most comprehensive statement about first-year curricula may be found in the WPA Outcomes Statement, adopted by the Council of Writing Program Administrators in April 2000, and posted on the organization's website. Given the variety of approaches to the content of the course, a focus on student outcomes as a unifying feature of first-year composition makes good sense. The specific outcomes are listed under four areas: Rhetorical Knowledge; Critical Thinking, Reading, and Writing; Processes; and Knowledge of Conventions. These outcomes are not meant to be standards (that is, precise levels of achievement), but simply a way of regularizing first-year writing courses by identifying those features that all in the field can agree upon. The Council encourages WPAs to take the outcomes statement and adapt it to suit their own particular institutions and student demographics.

Basic Writing

A WPA will often be called upon to develop a curriculum for under-prepared students for a course that precedes first-year composition.[2] Although this sort of course used to be (and sometimes still is) referred to as "remedial," the term developed by Mina Shaughnessy to describe the wave of non-traditional students who arrived as a result of open admissions is the one now most commonly used: basic writing. Shaughnessy's book *Errors and Expectations: A Guide for the Teacher of Basic Writing,* published in1977, was the first book to speak to the issues these writers have; it covers such issues as handwriting and punctuation, syntax, common errors, spelling, vocabulary, issues beyond the sentence level, and finally, a chapter entitled "Expectations" in which she reminds readers that the "expectations of learners and teachers powerfully influence what happens in school" and that "not all students who have been judged academically inferior are necessarily or natively so" (275).

A useful resource for developing curricula for basic writers is *A Source Book for Basic Writing Teachers,* edited by Theresa Enos. The book is divided into three parts: "Contexts for Basic Writing Teachers," "Theories for Basic Writing Teachers, " and "Strategies for Basic

Writing Teachers," along with a series of bibliographies. The piece by David Bartholomae and Anthony Petrosky in this book is taken from their book *Facts, Artifacts and Counterfacts: A Basic Reading and Writing Course for the College Curriculum*, which describes a curriculum that set the standard for many basic writing courses by assuming that the best way to engage all writers, including basic writers, is through intellectually challenging material rather than through workbooks and drill. Classroom materials are included in the book. A more recent book is Marcia Dickson's *It's Not Like That Here: Teaching Academic Writing and Reading to Novice Writers*, which provides advice on devising a curriculum that asks students to research a topic about which they have some experience, integrating library work with ethnographic research in order to introduce them to the genre of academic writing.

The *Bedford Bibliography for Teachers of Basic Writing* (Adler-Kassner and Glau) describes these and other resources for curriculum development (this book is also available on line). This bibliography was compiled by members of the Conference on Basic Writing (CBW), a special-interest group of the Conference on College Composition and Communication, now in its twenty-fifth year. Other sections of the book deal with the history and theory of basic writing, pedagogical issues, and administrative issues. *The Journal of Basic Writing*, sponsored by the CBW with support from the City University of New York, is also a useful resource for planning curricula for basic writing courses. Sometimes students with learning disabilities appear in basic writing classes, often undiagnosed. FAME (Faculty and Administrator Modules in Higher Education) is an online program developed by The Ohio State University; these modules are designed to take both faculty and administrators through best practices with regard to these students. The modules may be found on the Ohio State website.

Discussions of basic writing invariably turn to issues of grammar, but it is also an issue for all writing classes. Because so many outside the discipline think of writing in terms of correctness, grammar is an issue that cannot simply be ignored. Patrick Hartwell's essay "Grammar, Grammars, and the Teaching of Grammar" is an excellent introduction to the fraught issue of grammar in the composition class; he points out that although it seems clear that students do not learn to write by studying grammar rules, the issue is in fact rather complex, since there are a number of different things people mean when they use the term "grammar," including those issues teachers often ask students to address as they edit their penultimate drafts. Constance Weaver's *Teaching Grammar in Context,* discusses the place of grammar and related issues of usage and mechanics in the writing class.

ESL and Generation 1.5 Students

Students who speak English as a second language need a curriculum that requires a somewhat different approach, perhaps even a separate class. Dana Ferris discusses these needs in *Treatment of Error in Second Language Student Writing,* focusing on how to teach such students self-editing strategies. In *Teaching ESL Composition: Purpose, Process, and Practice,* she and her co-author John Hedgcock discuss theoretical and practical issues in ESL writing, the reading-writing relationship for ESL writers, syllabus design, text selection, lesson planning, teacher and peer response to student's writing (including the place of grammar in the editing process), writing assessment and ESL writers, and the implications of computer-assisted writing for ESL writers. Barbara Kroll's *Exploring the Dynamics of Second Language Writing* has several essays that focus on curriculum options for ESL/EFL writing classes, including discussions of the connection between reading and writing and the assigning of literature in such classes. Plagiarism is sometimes a concern with ESL students, given different cultural attitudes toward the ownership of written text and the availability of electronic texts. In Diane Belcher and Alan Hirvela's *Linking Literacies: Perspectives on L2 Reading-Writing Connections,* there is a section entitled "[E]Merging Literacies and the Challenge of Textual Ownership" that includes three articles on the subject, discussing the varied attitudes of international students toward Western citation practices and advice on curricula, warning against penalties for inadvertent plagiarism among this group of students. *Writing in Multicultural Settings* (Severino et al.) contains a section on ESL issues, including an essay by Tony Silva on the implications of research on the differences between ESL writers and native speakers, as well as other sections having to do with linguistic and cultural diversity in the writing classroom, especially with regard to students of color.

In many institutions there is now another group of students for whom an ESL class is not appropriate, since they are very proficient orally, showing second-language interference only in their writing. These are students who were born in the U.S. or came with their families when they were very young and have received most or all of their education here, speaking English at school and another language at home. Their language profiles fall somewhere between the recent immigrant or international student and a native speaker of English; they are termed "Generation 1.5" as a result. Volume 14.1 of the *CATESOL Journal* (2002) has one section devoted to these students. The lead article, "Working with Generation 1.5 Students and their Teachers: ESL Meets Composition" (Goen et al.), describes a research project that has identified a number of successful curricular practice for such students: using meaningful texts that are relevant to students, making basic grammar succinct and accessible, and helping students develop editing strategies that are very focused and individualized (150). The essay includes a helpful appendix that outlines a series of principles for teachers working with orally proficient second-language writers, along with examples of the sorts of activities that can be integrated into a curriculum for these students.

Articulation

Discussions of curriculum often involve discussions of articulation with feeder schools (that is, whether or not to accept composition courses at other institutions as equivalent to your own school's course) and outreach to high schools, to build collaborative programs that facilitate the transition from school to college. In "Expanding the Community: A Comprehensive Look at Outreach and Articulation," Anne-Marie Hall discusses various outreach programs, focusing particularly on high school-college cooperation. She cites the National Writing Project as a model, but also discusses mounting graduate seminars and institutes, bridge programs, young writers programs, and cooperative teaching programs, providing practical advice about the challenges of designing such programs. She also provides a list of resources, including Web sites, that give the most current sources of information about setting up and evaluating an outreach program.

Beyond First-Year Composition

Although the present reference guide focuses primarily on first-year composition, a writing program administrator will often be called upon to design courses beyond the introductory course, or at least to articulate that course with other courses at the sophomore or upper-division level. The curriculum of "advanced" writing courses varies considerably across institutions. The variations were the subject of essays in the early years of *JAC: Journal of Advanced Composition* (which now carries the subtitle "A Journal of Writing Theory"); there are also examples of course designs that have appeared since Fall 1997 as a regular feature of *Composition Studies.* The most comprehensive collection of essays and course designs may be found in Shamoon et al., *Coming of Age: The Advanced Writing Curriculum,* which comes with an interactive CD-ROM that provides full course descriptions for each type of course discussed in the book. In the introduction to the book, Shamoon and her colleagues discuss the difficulty of defining what constitutes "advanced composition," since much of what comes under that rubric seems to have been "left over from a period in which advanced undergraduate writing instruction was either very specialized (e.g., technical writing), an extension of the literature curriculum (the non-fiction essay), or an extension of first-year composition (more of the same, but harder)" (xiv). Choosing instead to focus on what an advanced writing curriculum should or could accomplish, Shamoon and her colleagues recommend three curricular objectives: providing students with a historical and theoretical awareness of writing as a discipline, preparing students for careers as writers, and preparing students to use writing to participate in the civic sphere—what they term the disciplinary, the professional, and the public (xv). The book describes and gives examples of various core courses in each of these three areas.

Pedagogy

As documented in Lad Tobin's "How the Writing Process Movement Was Born," the 1970s marked what has become known as the "process revolution" in composition pedagogy, ushered in by, for example, Donald Murray ("Teach Writing As A Process" and *A Writer Teaches Writing*) and Peter Elbow (*Writing without Teachers*). This revolution in teaching was brought about in part because of the larger national conversation about teaching and learning, sparked by the launching of Sputnik in 1957, but was also based on the intuitive notion on the part of such writers as Murray and Elbow that we should teach students to write the way that we ourselves write, going through multiple drafts and asking for feedback from peers. Linda Flower and John Hayes sought to confirm this intuition in their empirical research at Carnegie Mellon, comparing the writing processes of expert and novice writers. Pat Belanoff and Peter Elbow (among others) developed a portfolio system for assessing student writing that honored the process of writing as well as the finished product. Although current-traditional approaches to pedagogy still exist, scholars in the field generally agree that best practices include careful assignment design (with attention to invention strategies and rhetorical context and including evaluative critera), multiple drafts, collaborative work with peers/peer review, and portfolio evaluation (about which more will be said later). Most important, the role of the teacher is seen as one of coach as well as judge, of guide as well as critic. This change in pedagogy has been great enough that it has been termed a "paradigm shift" (Hairston "Winds of Change").

In 1986, George Hillocks published the results of a meta-analysis of experimental research having to do with the teaching of composition, *Research on Written Composition: New Directions for Teaching*. The study examined four modes of instruction: "presentational" (where the teacher dominates the classroom), "natural process" (in which students choose their own topics, receive feedback from peers, and revise as they wish, with no structured problem-solving), "individualized writing conferences" (between teacher and student), and "environmental" (an approach that balances teacher, student, materials, activities, and learning tasks, and that uses small group discussions that are focused, using specific criteria to give feedback on papers, for example). He found that students who were taught using the environmental approach significantly out-performed their counterparts in the other modes of instruction. His later book, *Teaching Writing as Reflective Practice,* draws on this research as well as on theories of language and learning; after outlining basics for thinking about teaching writing, he devotes the rest of the book to describing successful environmental approaches, discussing the process model of composing, and giving practical advice about planning the course, including what he calls "gateway" (beginning) activities, sequencing of assignments, and the place of reflection in planning and teaching. Although the book is aimed primarily at middle school and secondary teachers, the synthesis of research and theory and the discussions of general teaching and learning principles are all applicable to college-level teaching.

The most recent book outlining various pedagogical approaches is *A Guide to Composition Pedagogies* (Tate et al.); the first essay, by Lad Tobin, provides a comprehensive overview of process pedagogy, including critiques of early expressivist notions as the focus of the field turned toward teaching academic discourse, and the recent discussions of "post-process" pedagogy that focus on what the content of a writing course should be. There are also essays on expressivist pedagogy (Christopher Burnham), collaborative pedagogy (Rebecca Moore Howard), cultural studies and composition (Diana George and John Trimbur), critical pedagogy (Ann George), feminist pedagogy (Susan C. Jarratt), community service pedagogy (Laura Julier), basic writing pedagogy (Deborah Mutnick), and an essay on technology and teaching writing (Charles Moran).[3]

Moran's essay discusses one of the most important recent developments in composition pedagogy, the emergence of multiple literacies, including electronic literacy. The essay provides an overview of sources and a useful section on various applications of technology, including word processing, electronic mail, online discussions, the Web/hypertext/hypermedia, and a section on the various issues that are raised by the applications of computer technology (most important, perhaps, the issue of access). Moran also provides a bibliography of both print and (of course) online resources. For information on the history of computers and composition, the standard references are *Computers and the Teaching of Writing in American Higher Education, 1979–1994: A History* (Hawisher et al.), and the more recent *Transitions: Teaching Writing in Computer-Supported and Traditional Classrooms* (Palmquist et al.), the latter of which contains an extensive bibliography of related readings. Two journals, the online *Kairos* and the print/online *Computers and Composition,* provide the most recent scholarship on technology and pedagogy in the writing class. Todd Taylor's "Ten Commandments for Computers and Composition" offers specific advice to WPAs on using technology in the writing classroom: keep people first, identify and build from program principles, start simple, invest heavily on hands-on instructor training, revise strategies for instructing students, consult with others, expect the crash, consider access, be critical of technology, and use technology for positive change.

In order to manage the individualized pedagogy required for a writing class, it is imperative that class size be kept small, ideally no more than 15 for basic writing and no more than 20 for regular first-year composition. The recommended standards for class size come from three national organizations: the National Council of Teachers of English, the Conference on College Composition and Communication, and the Association of Departments of English, an affiliate of the Modern Language Association. These guidelines, which are posted on the organizations' websites, make the argument for class size in terms of workload issues.

Assessment and Accountability

For WPAs, accountability is inextricably tied to assessment because WPAs are, by virtue of being in charge of what is often the only universal requirement in the institution, accountable to many stakeholders outside the department/program—faculty across the disciplines, administrators, boards of trustees/regents, and sometimes legislators. A good rule of thumb is what has become known informally among WPAs as "Ed White's Law "—assess, or assessment will be done unto you. The university runs on data; WPAs are usually called upon to provide data that show what and how the students and program are doing. There has been much research and scholarship focusing on assessment, only some of which pertains to administrative issues. After a discussion of general overviews of the topic, the following section will focus only on those resources that deal with the intersections of assessment and administrative accountability for the WPA: placement, proficiency, and program assessment.

Overviews

Kathleen Blake Yancey provides a history of writing assessment in "Looking Back as We Look Forward: Historicizing Writing Assessment." She traces three waves of such assessment: multiple-choice tests, holistically-scored essay tests, and portfolio assessment, showing the move toward direct assessment and what has come to be termed "authentic assessment" (e.g., assessment of collective abilities rather than isolated skills [like editing]). *On a Scale: A Social History of Writing Assessment in America* (Elliot) provides a more comprehensive examination of the topic, starting with the first Harvard writing examinations in 1874; he traces what he terms "three master diachronic tropes in the history of writing assessment: an impulse for accountability recorded as student disenfranchisement, a struggle for methodological design resulting in a series of case studies, and a construction of literacy that varies across time and circumstance" (348). In his chapter "Using Tests for Admissions, Placement, and Instructional

Evaluation," Edward White provides an overview of the purposes of these various types of tests: admissions, placement, first-year composition equivalency, exit from composition courses (including Advanced Placement and CLEP), certification of "rising junior" or graduation writing competency, and demonstration of "value added" (e.g., proof of academic improvement for students or groups of students over time) for program evaluation ("Developing"). He points out that each of these has two (sometimes conflicting) goals—administrative (selecting and classifying students) and instructional (helping students learn more effectively)—and each requires a different sort of assessment. Further, any assessment instrument needs to be context-specific; a basic writer at one institution might not be defined as such at another (118).

A more recent overview is Huot and Schendel's "A Working Methodology of Assessment for Writing Program Administrators," an essay that provides an extensive bibliography on the topic. These authors discuss the potential positive force of assessment mandates, as long as they are done in a way that allow WPAs to work effectively and ethically. They define the terms "reliability" and "validity," and outline methods of assessment and the theories behind them, discussing placement and exit assessments and program assessments. They point out the importance of first establishing the validity of any writing assessment, and recommend bringing in experts to help with designing site-specific assessment instruments.

Willa Wolcott and Sue M. Legg's *An Overview of Writing Assessment: Theory, Research, and Practice,* is just that. The authors provide chapters on direct measures of writing (that is, measures that examine student writing, as opposed to indirect measures—multiple-choice questions about editing, for example), topic design for writing assessment, portfolio assessment, training of raters, holistic, primary trait, and analytic scoring, reliability and validity, assessing writing in the disciplines, and issues of equity in writing assessment. In *The Testing Trap: How State Writing Assessments Control Learning,* George Hillocks gives an overview of how state mandated assessments have become politicized; although this book focuses on K-12 assessments, what is said about the difficulties of large-scale assessments that are divorced from instruction (and how assessment can drive instruction in negative ways) also applies to post-secondary education. Recently various commercial vendors have been offering assessment packages that include computer scoring of student writing, packages that appeal to upper administrators because of their perceived efficiency and comparative costs. Anne Herrington and Charles Moran give an overview of such scoring ("What Happens When Machines Read Our Students' Writing?"), pointing out, among other things, how easy it is to fool the machines. Richard Haswell provides an extensive bibliography of resources on computer scoring of writing in his book with Patricia Freitag Ericsson, *Machine Scoring of Student Essays*. The Conference on College Composition and Communication has developed a Position Statement on Teaching, Learning, and Assessing Writing in Digital Environments that opposes machine scoring of student writing.

Placement

In his chapter "Selecting Appropriate Measures," Edward White outlines the case against using indirect measures, especially standardized tests from commercial vendors ("Teaching"). The issue, White argues, is fairness as well as an accurate assessment of student skills; he discusses the results of a study that compared the English Placement Test (EPT, offered by the California State University system) and the Test of Standard Written English (TSWE, a test no longer offered by the College Board). Black students and Asian American students did significantly better on the EPT, a direct measure, than on the TSWE; White theorized that one reason for this outcome was that the standardized test penalized non-significant features of minority dialects and the language of students whose home language was not English (188–91). White advises those designing placement instruments to first decide what information is needed for placement in such courses; only then can one proceed to designing an appropriate instrument. The next chapter in his book describes how to go about organizing and managing holistic essay readings or portfolio readings for that purpose. Holistic scoring, first developed by at team at the Educational Testing Service, is perhaps the most common method of scoring placement examinations. Leo Ruth and Sandra Murphy's *Designing Writing Tasks for the Assessment of Writing* and Michael Williamson and Brian Huot's *Validating Holistic Scoring for Writing Assessment: Theoretical and Empirical Foundations* are resources for designing and scoring such examinations.

A more streamlined system for such scoring was developed independently by William Smith at the University of Pittsburgh and

Richard Haswell and his colleagues at Washington State University. In "Assessing the Reliability and Adequacy of Using Holistic Scoring of Essays as a College Composition Placement Technique," Smith reviews the research up to that time (1993) on direct vs. indirect measures, and describes the modifications he made to holistic scoring, which he terms "placement rating." Instead of having raters score writing samples according to a scale of 1–6, this system relies on experienced teachers to rate the essays based on the curricula for each course students will be placed into. A similar "expert reader" model is described by Richard Haswell in "The Two-Tier Rating System: The Need for Ongoing Change" and "The Obvious Placement: The Addition of Theory," both in his book *Beyond Outcomes: Assessment and Instruction Within a University Writing Program*. Haswell's system relies on a two-tiered reading: the first by experienced teachers of both basic writing and first-year composition; the sample that suggests an "obvious placement" is not read again. Only the papers that are not so clear in terms of placement go to a second more experienced reader. The newest direction in placement is directed self-placement, described in detail in Daniel Royer and Roger Gilles' book *Directed Self-Placement: Principles and Practice*. In such a placement system, students are given information and advice about the placement options (e.g., if you are this sort of reader/writer, this course is the most appropriate for you), but the ultimate decision about placement rests with the student. One major advantage of this system, as they point out, is that student motivation in the basic writing class is not a difficult issue because the students have chosen to take the class rather than having been forced to take it.

Proficiency

Placement tests ask an entry-level question: what writing course is most appropriate for this student, given his/her level of skill? Holistically scored timed writing is a narrow but appropriate measure to get at the answer to this question. Proficiency tests, on the other hand, ask a gatekeeping question: has this student achieved a level of skill to be able to pass first-year composition/go on to junior standing/graduate? To answer the second question, an assessment instrument must be based on the intended outcomes of the course, measuring how well students have achieved those outcomes. Portfolios have become the most common instruments for measuring students' progress in process-oriented courses. Pat Belanoff and Peter Elbow pioneered portfolios as measures of proficiency; their system is described in a series of essays in *Portfolios: Process and Product* (Belanoff and Dickson). The system as they describe it has become not only a method of certifying students' writing proficiency, but also a method of faculty development; it relies on groups of teachers reading each others' students' work, hammering out agreement on collective standards. An entire section of this book deals with issues of using portfolios for proficiency testing, including case studies of such testing at various institutions. *New Directions in Portfolio Assessment: Reflective Practice, Critical Theory, and Large-Scale Scoring* (Black et al.) also has a section devoted to the large-scale use of portfolios for assessing proficiency, focusing on issues of scoring. Edward White has reviewed the difficulties with scoring portfolios using holistic methods, proposing instead that the scoring focus on the students' reflective letter (a usual component of portfolios). Such a system requires first that the program have a clear statement of goals (he includes sample goals statements from four different programs in an appendix); the evaluators can then determine, based on a careful reading of the reflective letter, how well the student has achieved those goals ("The Scoring of Portfolios: Phase 2"). Digital portfolios, the latest development in portfolio assessment, are reviewed in *Electronic Portfolios: Emerging Practices in Student, Faculty, and Institutional Learning,* edited by Barbara Cambridge, and in the fourth section of Yancey and Weiser's *Situating Portfolios: Four Perspectives.*

Program Assessment

As Stephen Witte and Lester Faigley showed in their 1983 discussion of program assessment, *Evaluating College Writing Programs*, program evaluation involves much more than simply asking the question of whether or not student writing has improved. After reviewing four studies conducted at different institutions, they outlined a framework for a comprehensive evaluation that would include five components: cultural and social context, institutional context, program structure and administration, content or curriculum, and instruction (40–65). At about the same time, Barbara Davis and her colleagues in the Bay Area Writing Project were working on an evaluation of that project funded by the Carnegie Corporation; their work was first published in 1981 in a volume entitled *The Evaluation of Composition Instruction,* and although it focused primarily on the effects of the BAWP on subsequent instruction, it also provided useful guidelines that could be applied to program evaluation (for example, looking at student and teacher attitudes as well as program administration). In *Developing Successful College Writing Programs,* Edward White discusses program evaluation in some detail, suggesting that reducing it to a "value added" (popular in the late 1980s, when he was writing) was ineffective and inappropriate (195). He admits, reluctantly, that university administrators are likely to see "empirical" evaluations as the only ones that are convincing (197–98), and points to the failure of the studies cited by Witte and Faigley as examples of how difficult empirical studies can be. He has three recommendations: Learn from the past (e.g., from the empirical studies that have not worked), use multiple measures, and emphasize formative rather than summative evaluation (204). As an appendix, he adds the guidelines for the self-study that precedes the Consultant-Evaluator visit from the Council of Writing Program Administrators, a service behind which White has been a driving force. This service, information about which is available on the WPA Website, was started (as mentioned in the previous chapter) by Harvey Wiener, the founding president of WPA, who used his experience as an evaluator for the Middle States Association of Colleges and Schools. It remains the single most valuable program evaluation tool available to WPAs.

An example of a comprehensive and ongoing program evaluation may be found in Richard Haswell's collection of essays, *Beyond Outcomes: Assessment and Instruction in a University Writing Program.* Haswell and his colleagues at Washington State University describe the history of the writing program there, which includes the writing-across-the-curriculum program, the assessment instruments (a timed writing for placement, which provides baseline data, and a portfolio that includes a timed writing for the rising junior portfolio, which provides mid-point diagnostic data) and the feedback loop that the assessment provides back to the program. By comparing selected students' work on the placement examination and on the timed writing for the portfolio, Haswell provided a striking example of how to do what earlier programs (as documented by Witte and Faigley) had failed to do: use empirical methods to show improvement in student writing ("Documenting Improvement in College Writing: A Longitudinal Approach").

Staffing, Staff Development, and Evaluation

Of all the issues facing WPAs, staffing has been and remains the thorniest. Although there are some institutions where only full-time permanent faculty teach composition, the vast majority of first-year writing courses are taught by contingent faculty and teaching assistants, many of them professionally unprepared to teach such a course. Kathleen Blake Yancey and her colleagues, in their survey of writing faculty, found that of 1,861 respondents from all institutional types (40 percent were at two-year institutions, the remainder at various kinds of four-year schools) only 27 percent indicated that they had a background in rhetoric and composition; 33 percent had a background in literature, 15 percent indicated "other," with the rest in various fields (e.g., linguistics, English education) ("Portraits"). Further, the pedagogy of writing classes (requiring small sections) combined with the budget structure of some institutions (tied to enrollments), creates situations where last-minute hiring is the norm—for introductory science and mathematics classes, 20 more first-year students over the expected number of enrollments may simply require a larger lecture hall, but for first-year writing classes, that enrollment upsurge requires one more section and one more person to teach it. Providing quality instruction under such circumstances becomes a challenge.

As mentioned earlier, the National Council of Teachers of English, the Conference on College Composition and Communication, and the Association of Departments of English have responded to the issue of staffing with various policy statements meant to support a high quality of instruction. These guidelines collectively indicate that writing classes be capped at no more than 15 for basic writing and no more than 20 for first-year composition; they further recommend that no teacher of writing have more than 60 students to work with per term. Hilgers and Marsella, in Chapter 3 of *Making Your Writing Program Work,* advise that every program should have a clear staffing plan that takes into account these professional constraints, including the "Principles and Standards for the Postsecondary Teaching of Writing" (the Position Statement from the Conference on College Composition and Communication), as well as institutional and legal constraints (such as Affirmative Action/Equal Employment Opportunity guidelines). They recommend establishing a personnel committee for the program, an ongoing staff development program to upgrade the professionalism of the faculty, looking for professional staff in non-academic areas for particular needs (for example, a business executive to teach business writing), and finding ways to make the positions attractive if the pay is low (providing flexible work hours or travel money).

Hilgers and Marsella also describe the hiring process in detail, from recruitment to sealing the deal. They go on in Chapter 4 to give advice on organizing faculty development programs to fit institutional and faculty needs, including a seminar for writing-intensive courses in the disciplines as well as one for new hires. This chapter also deals with performance evaluations of teachers. Edward White's *Developing Successful College Writing Programs* devotes Chapter 8 to the discussion of supporting, evaluating, and rewarding writing program faculty. White emphasizes the importance of providing a manageable student load for teachers, as well as supporting their professional growth. William J. Carpenter discusses strategies for professional development of staff, including writing reviews of textbooks, forming discussion groups, and holding in-house conferences. Christine Hult's *Evaluating Teachers of Writing* provides a series of essays that give an overview of the topic (how does one evaluate such teaching?), a discussion of various evaluation methods, and an examination of various faculty groups (including TAs, adjuncts, and faculty in writing-across-the-curriculum programs) and how to evaluate them.

At doctoral and comprehensive institutions (e.g., those that offer MA degrees), graduate teaching assistants usually comprise the largest group of staff teaching first-year writing classes. This is a group that presents particular challenges, since the position of TA elsewhere in the institution is understood as a true assistant—one who grades papers and perhaps leads a discussion section, but is not the teacher of record for the class. TAs in writing programs, however, are entirely responsible for their own sections, often from the creation of the syllabus to giving final grades. Because of this difference, some institutions have instituted graduate seminars in writing pedagogy, required of TAs either before they teach or concurrently with their first teaching term, or practicum courses that provide support during their novice period. Responses to a recent query on the WPA Listserv indicated that the most commonly used books for such courses were Roen et al.'s *Strategies for Teaching First-Year Composition*, Clark's *Concepts in Composition*, Glenn et al.'s *The St Martin's Guide to Teaching Writing*,

Corbett et al.'s *The Writing Teacher's Sourcebook,* and Lindemann's *A Rhetoric for Writing Teachers.*

Timothy Catalano and his colleagues have put together a useful annotated bibliography of resources for TA training, first published in *WPA: Writing Program Administration* and reprinted in Ward and Carpenter's *Allyn & Bacon Sourcebook for Writing Program Administrators;* the bibliography has sections on TA training and evaluation, descriptions of training programs, teaching duties, employment issues, and histories of TA training. Ward and Carpenter's book also includes two other essays on TA training that provide overviews of relevant issues and practices: Ward and Perry's "A Selection of Strategies for Training Teaching Assistants" (which provides a bibliography of additional resources) and Latterell's "Training the Workforce: Overview of GTA Education Curricula."

The most complete reference on TA training is Pytlik and Liggett's *Preparing College Teachers of Writing,* a collection of essays that focus on the histories, theories, programs, and practices involved in TA training. One essay by Stephen Wilhoit, "Recent Trends in TA Instruction," is a bibliographic essay that traces trends in three areas:

1. Program structure (longer and more extensive pre-service programs, in-service practica with more emphasis on theory, apprenticeship and mentorship programs with more experienced teachers, training TAs to tutor in a writing center);

2. Trends in program practices and content (classroom observations, role-playing, teaching journals and portfolios, encouraging reflective practice and research and publication, teaching about writing program administration);

3. Trends in employment concerns and working conditions for TAs, including unionization.

Administrative and Professional Issues

Faculty members can operate fairly well without knowing what goes on outside of their home department, but once they become administrators they need to know how the university is structured and where the lines of authority lie. There is a vast amount of literature in the larger field of higher education administration that can be helpful to new WPAs in this regard. Jossey-Bass publishes a series of books called "New Directions for Higher Education"; a good general reference is Birnbaum's *How Colleges Work: the Cybernetics of Academic Organization and Leadership.* Some of the issues new WPAs will deal with are understanding administrative discourse and budgets, legal issues, the politics of WPA work, their own tenure and promotion process, and—on a more personal level—how to handle the stress of administrative work.

Administrative discourse can take some getting used to. Doug Hesse offers a list of periodicals and references that university administrators read and discuss in "Understanding Larger Discourses in Higher Education: Practical Advice for WPAs." Hesse recommends that WPAs familiarize themselves with these periodicals and with various organizations that focus on higher education (such as the American Council on Education, the Association of Governing Boards of Universities and Colleges, and the Association of American Colleges and Universities). Understanding the larger conversations can help WPAs tie their own local initiatives to broader national initiatives or agendas (assessment, for example). Joyce Kinkead and Jeanne Simpson offer advice on decoding Adminispeak in "The Administrative Audience: A Rhetorical Problem." They discuss administrative shorthand terms such as FTE (full-time equivalent) and SCH (student credit hour), as well as terms like productivity and accountability—terms that have particular meanings in university contexts. For understanding budget issues, there are such reference guides as Born's *The Jossey-Bass Academic Administrator's Guide to Budget and Financial Management,* which gives a general background on managing academic budgets. Chris Anson's "Figuring it Out: Writing Programs in the Context of University Budgets" gives more specific information on how writing program budgets work, pointing out that each university has its own budgeting process and idiosyncrasies; Anson describes a process of mapping budgets as a heuristic for understanding them.

The WPA is part of an administrative line of authority, which can in some cases result in liability; legal issues are crucial to understand, especially before the WPA meets up with that student who has the number of her father—the lawyer—on her cell phone's speed dial. Goonen and Blechman's *Higher Education Administration: A Guide to Legal, Ethical, and Practical Issues* provides an overview of both legal and ethical concerns. Pantoja et al.'s "Legal Considerations for Writing Program Administrators" outlines the major concerns that WPAs deal with: contracts and who can sign them, syllabi and their legal status as contracts, disruptive behavior and student rights, sexual harassment, student records and FERPA (the Family Educational Rights and Privacy Act, which does not allow one to discuss a student's records with his or her parents without the student's permission), plagiarism and the proof required, copyright issues, responsibilities with regard to disclosures by students, hiring practices and personnel evaluations, letters of recommendation, and accommodating students with disabilities. The essay includes a listing of resources for each of these issues. Ethical concerns are addressed in Stuart Brown's "Applying Ethics: A Decision-Making Heuristic for Writing Program Administrators." Brown provides a series of common scenarios for WPAs (hiring part-time faculty at the last minute, dealing with TAs who deviate from the standard syllabus) and outlines a moral heuristic for helping to make decisions in such contexts. The heuristic involves mapping out "matters of fact" and "matters of consequence," the most important of which is probably "Based on my own personal values, can I live with this decision?" (161).

The politics of writing program administration within and outside of English Departments are always highly nuanced. In "The WPA and the Politics of LitComp," John Schilb discusses English Departments' traditional marginalizing of composition. Citing William Riley Parker's famous essay, "Where Do English Departments Come From?" and Maxine Hairston's "Breaking Our Bonds and Reaffirming Our Connections," Schilb discusses what he terms "our vexed disciplinary history" (167) and gives advice about basic decisions WPAs must make about the relationship of the writing program to literature: What part will literature play in the curriculum? Who should the instructors in the program be? How should the graduate students be chosen and trained? How can you make sure that your literature colleagues understand and appreciate your work? Barry Maid discusses the advantages of moving entirely outside of the English Department to form a separate unit for the writing program ("Working Outside of English"). In "Politics and the WPA," Doug Hesse outlines some of the larger political issues involved, advising WPAs to know the system in which they operate, develop written policies and create processes, construct an effective ethos (one that combines expertise, competence, sensitivity to local issues, and pursuit of the greater good), and write strategic reports. At the institutional level he offers these maxims: have a place at the table (even if the table is small), know the other participants, come to the parties (such as guest lectures and football games), and frame strategies by factoring in the resource situation. At the disciplinary level, he advises that WPAs be familiar with previous and ongoing political activities (such as official statements); become involved in local, regional, and national political efforts; and seek professional sponsorship for actions (such as the development of the "Outcomes Statement"). Finally, at the higher education/public sphere level, he advises that writing program administrators shape public opinion through speaking and writing, form coalitions, and have a place at larger tables (state-wide task forces, for example).

Tenure and promotion has been and in some cases still continues to be an issue for WPAs, since their administrative work is not always appreciated or understood as scholarship by their department colleagues or by personnel committees and deans. The Council of Writing Program Administrators position statement on evaluating the intellectual work of the WPA was created precisely because of this situation. In "Professional Advancement of the WPA: Rhetoric and Politics in Tenure and Promotion," Jeanne Gunner gives advice about how to achieve tenure and discusses her own promotion and tenure case, showing how she revised her materials after a shaky probationary review. She includes an extensive annotated bibliography with the essay. Charles Schuster, in "The Politics of Promotion," outlines how English departments should take responsibility for educating faculty about the work of the writing program administrator, sponsoring faculty colloquia, re-evaluating teaching loads and the importance of teaching, hiring assistant professors in rhetoric and composition as specialists and colleagues, and assigning the job of WPA to a senior writing specialist. The most complete general reference on tenure and promotion is Richard and Barbara Gebhardt's *Academic Advancement in Composition Studies,* which includes essays on preparing for a successful personnel review, mentoring and finding mentors, and the importance of external reviews. The most immediately relevant essay is Duane Roen's "Writing Program Administration as Scholarship and Teaching." Roen provides a case study that demonstrates some of the issues involved, and then discusses the need for fair evaluation standards of the kind of work WPAs do, focusing on the need for complete job descriptions and a mapping out of the administrative work that counts as scholarship or teaching (rather than service) in Ernest Boyer's terms (in *Scholarship Reconsidered*).

Finally but foremost, WPAs need to take care of themselves. Administrative work can be stressful; some stress is energizing, but too much can be debilitating. Irene Ward discusses this issue in "Developing Healthy Management and Leadership Styles: Surviving the WPA's 'Inside Game.'" Ward defines burnout, discusses the issues that may lead to burnout in WPA positions, and outlines strategies to avoid it. She gives very specific advice: get a reasonable job description and have an annual review with your chair/supervisor, involve others and build teams (empowering others to act effectively), seek out positive role models, negotiate for the training you need (for supervision, leadership, and management), develop realistic expectations, find ways to minimize interruptions that interfere with your duties, balance your life with interests outside work, stop thinking you are a victim and take control, and create a list of deal-breakers (those things that would make your position so difficult that you would step down). Ward closes her essay with a discussion of new management and leadership theories that should resonate with WPAs. Quoting from several books on management theory, she states that these theories are based on mutual respect, understanding, and empowerment, and speak of leadership as teaching and learning. Noting that WPAs often have to teach the university how to treat them, she states that we also need to prepare new WPAs to face the challenges of the job. With a clear understanding of what to expect, the work of the WPA can be energizing, fulfilling, and effective.

5 Glossary

Each institution has its own acronyms and terminology; the following is intended to be suggestive rather than comprehensive.

AAC & U—American Association of Colleges and Universities. A national organization founded in 1915 that focuses on undergraduate liberal education. The organization publishes several periodicals, including *Liberal Education* and *Peer Review,* and sponsors various initiatives for improving undergraduate education.

AAUP—American Association of University Professors. Founded by John Dewey and Arthur O. Lovejoy in 1915, the organization's purpose is "to advance academic freedom and shared governance, to define fundamental professional values and standards for higher education, and to ensure higher education's contribution to the common good" (www.aaup.org).

Academic rank and title—Tenure-track faculty usually progress through a fairly rigid set of ranks. At most institutions, new colleagues just out of graduate school are hired as assistant professors and are considered "junior" faculty. After a specific probationary period of time in rank, usually six years, they must be considered for tenure and promotion to associate professor. The position of full professor may or may not be achieved, depending on a faculty member's contributions to the field and department as well as time in rank. Associate and full professors are considered "senior" faculty. The titles of "instructor" and "lecturer" usually refer to non-tenure-track faculty. The title of "administrative professional" is sometimes used to designate an administrative staff position outside faculty ranks, and is sometimes used for WPA positions. Depending on the context, this job classification can be problematic for WPAs because it puts them outside the faculty ranks.

Accountability—The responsibility of reporting to stakeholders outside the university (taxpayers, governing boards, legislators) about how the institution is fulfilling its mission and meeting its goals.

Accreditation—The process by which institutions are examined and approved to offer degrees, through the Council for Higher Education Accreditation, a non-profit organization of colleges and universities. The accreditation process involves a self-study, a visit by an accreditation team, and follow-up. Because the accreditation process examines (among other things) an institution's general education program, writing programs are or should be involved in the review.

ADA—Americans with Disabilities Act. This act, passed in 1990, requires institutions to provide "reasonable accommodation" for students with documented disabilities, including learning disabilities. A WPA may be called upon to work out reasonable accommodations for such students with their teachers. The ADA home page is http://www.usdoj.gov/crt/ada/adahom1.htm.

ADE—Association of Departments of English. An organization for chairs of English Departments and humanities divisions, sponsored by the Modern Language Association. ADE holds summer seminars for chairs and publishes information of general interest to chairs in the *ADE Bulletin* and *Profession* magazine. The organization also conducts surveys (about, for example, job placement rates for new PhDs) and publishes the results.

AP—Advanced placement. AP credit is granted for classes on the basis of scores achieved on standardized examinations sponsored by the College Board. The two AP courses that offer credit for writing courses are English Language and English Literature. The grades range from 1 (no recommendation) to 5 (very well qualified). Some schools give credit for first-year composition to students achieving a 3 or above (more than half of those taking the test in 2003 achieved that level, according to College Board statistics).

Articulation agreement—An agreement about how general education courses will count for transfer students. Public four-year institutions often have agreements that an academic Associate of Arts degree from particular community colleges guarantees that students will have fulfilled most or all lower-division general education requirements, including the writing requirement.

Glossary

Assessment—It is important to distinguish among various sorts of assessment. Diagnostic assessment's purpose is to discover, before instruction, the students' skill levels and abilities in order to provide appropriate instruction. Formative assessment's purpose is to support learning, providing feedback throughout instruction to help the student learn better (on successive drafts of papers, for example). Summative assessment's purpose is evaluative, summing up the progress the student has made at the end of a unit or term, usually in the form of a grade. See also "Program Evaluation."

Campaign—An organized fund-raising effort led by the Development Office, with a target amount to generate in gifts and pledges. See also "Development Office."

Carnegie classification—A classification system developed by the Carnegie Foundation to designate different sorts of higher education institutions. The first classification system was published in 1973 and has been updated several times since then. The classification established in 2000 was as follows:

- Doctorate-granting Institutions (Research-Extensive, granting 50 or more doctorates a year across at least 15 disciplines, and Research-Intensive, granting at least ten doctorates across at least three disciplines or at least 20 doctorates overall per year)
- Master's Colleges and Universities (MA I, granting at least 40 or more MAs across three or more disciplines, and MA II, granting at least 20 MAs per year.)
- Baccalaureate Colleges (Liberal Arts, General, and Baccalaureate/Associates)
- Associates Colleges (usually two-year institutions)
- Specialized Institutions (theological seminaries, medical schools, schools of engineering, business/management, music and art, law, teachers' colleges, etc.)
- Tribal Colleges and Universities

The classification system was updated in 2005 to provide a more dynamic method of categorizing institutions. See http://www.carnegiefoundation.org/classifications/index.asp?key=785.

Carnegie Foundation—The Carnegie Foundation for the Advancement of Teaching, founded in 1905 by Andrew Carnegie and chartered by Congress the next year. It is an independent research and policy entity focusing on the teaching profession and on higher education.

Carnegie unit—A standard unit developed in the early twentieth century to measure the amount of time a student studies a particular subject, originally to determine readiness for college: entering freshman were to have a minimum of 14 units (one subject, meeting four or five times a week for 40–60 minutes, 36 to 40 weeks a year for a minimum of 120 hours of total class time earned a student one unit of high school credit).

CCCC—Conference on College Composition and Communication, the national organization of college-level composition teachers; one must be a member of NCTE to join CCCC.

Chief Academic Officer (CAO)—The person in charge of the academic side of the university, usually the person also in charge of the academic budget. The title varies from institution (e.g., provost, academic vice president, executive vice chancellor); this is the person to whom the deans report. The president of the institution is the Chief Executive Officer (CEO), but in all but the smallest colleges the CEO is responsible for external issues (meeting with legislators or boards of governance, fund-raising), while the CAO is responsible for the day-to-day academic life of the institution.

Classified staff—Staff in various university classifications, most often support staff (non-faculty).

CLEP—College-Level Examination Program. CLEP offers examinations that are "equivalent" to college courses—general examinations, designed to meet general education requirements (all multiple-choice), and subject examinations, designed to meet specific requirements (which sometimes include optional essay portions). The CLEP examination in Composition comes in two versions, one of which is all multiple-choice, the other of which is multiple-choice with a short essay portion.

College Board—The College Entrance Examination Board, a nonprofit membership association founded in 1900 to standardize entrance requirements for colleges. The College Board is responsible for the SAT, CLEP, and Advanced Placement, among other exams. It contracts with other agencies, like the Educational Testing Service and Pearson, to develop and work out the scoring of these tests.

Committee structure—Most institutions have an established committee structure in place for policy and procedural matters; there us usually a university-wide personnel committee to make tenure recommendations, for example, and one to approve new courses or majors. It is important for a WPA to know how these committees work (e.g., how long it takes for a new course to get approved and listed in the catalog) and who serves on them.

Comparison institutions (or peer institutions)—The group of institutions to which a particular college or university compares itself in order to assess where it stands, often in the accreditation process. WPAs can make arguments to improve a writing program (e.g., for reducing class size) by appealing to best practices in comparison institutions.

Constituent institution—A university campus that is part of a larger collection of campuses within one system.

Contact hour—The amount of time students are actually in class with a teacher; one 50-minute class is one "contact hour." Working out equivalent contact hours (or "seat time") allows for accelerated classes, usually during summer session.

Development Office—The campus office in charge of fund-raising for the institution, sometimes also called Institutional Advancement. Get to know your development officer.

EOP—Educational Opportunity Program, a program that grew out of the Civil Rights Movement in late 1960s to provide support for students who had been excluded from higher education. Originally these were students of color; today EOP focuses on first-generation college students from low-income families.

ESL—English as a second language, often used with regard to international students, but also occasionally used for what have been termed "generation 1.5" students—those who have been born in the US or arrived when they were very young and who have attended school here, but who speak a language other than English at home. Linguists refer to L1 (the language spoken at home) and L2 (a second language). EFL (English as a foreign language) is the term sometimes used because English is often a learner's third or fourth language.

FERPA—Family Educational Rights and Privacy Act, also known as the Buckley Amendment, passed in 1974. The Act protects the privacy of university students. University officials cannot disclose information about a student's educational record to anyone, including parents, without written permission from the student.

FIPSE—Fund for the Improvement of Postsecondary Education. A federal grant program.

Fiscal year—July 1 to June 30, as opposed to the Academic year. Fiscal closing, which occurs June 30, requires that budgets be reconciled and all monies accounted for by that date. This is not a deadline that can be missed. Some budget categories allow money to be carried forward to the next fiscal year, while others require that the money be spent or returned before June 30. WPAs should have a ready list of things to purchase with funds in the latter category, since the realization that there is some money left often comes on June 29.

Foundation—The entity on some campuses that supports development or fund-raising activities and manages the funds donated to the institution. Extramural grants to the institution are often funded through the foundation or other similar office on campus; WPAs proposing extramural grants should check with this office before sending in any grant proposals, especially on budget issues.

FTE—Full-time equivalent, a way to count faculty (FTEF) or students (FTES). Two faculty members teaching half time equal one FTE; 15 FTE graduate teaching assistant appointments yields 30 half-time TAs.

GE (or GenEd)—General education, a program of breadth requirements for undergraduates which sometimes includes "core" required courses. First-year composition is nearly always a part of GE.

Goals statement—A statement that often follows a mission statement to further articulate the direction of the unit or institution.

HBCU—Historically Black colleges and universities.

HR—Human Resources, the office responsible for personnel management (such things as staff issues, employee and labor relations, benefits and retirement, workers' compensation, etc.)

IDEA—Individuals with Disabilities Education Improvement Act (2004), a law that works to improve educational results for children and youth with disabilities.

Glossary 111

Indirect costs—Money included in large extramural grants, over and above the amount requested for the proposed project, to cover overhead and services provided by the university. The money covers very real costs to the institution; depending on the institution and the granting agency, the indirect cost recovery may be 50 percent or more of the amount requested for the proposed project.

Institutional Assessment (or Institutional/University Research)—The office that compiles data and statistics on enrollments, retention rates, student/faculty ratios, and a host of other categories. It is the office responsible for generating data to be used by the upper administration in decision-making about resources (and therefore is sometimes part of the Office of Budget and Planning), and is a source of ready data for statistically-challenged WPAs.

IRB—Institutional Review Board, the entity responsible for reviewing research proposals for legal and ethical treatment of human subjects. Research involving students, faculty, or staff must be approved by the institution's IRB; if research is focused primarily on improving the educational experience of students, it may be exempt from human subjects regulations but must still be submitted for review.

Line item—A budget category, literally a single line on the budget. Faculty positions are usually line items, with permanent funding.

Mission statement—The statement that defines the goals of the institution, program, or unit.

MLA—Modern Language Association, the national organization for literature faculty in English and the modern foreign languages.

NASULGC—The National Association of State Universities and Land Grant Colleges. Founded in 1887, NASULGC is the nation's oldest higher education association, a voluntary association of public universities, land-grant institutions, and many of the nation's public university systems.

NCTE—The National Council of Teachers of English, the national organization for all English and language arts teachers, K-16, founded in 1911 by a group of teachers who broke away from the Modern Language Association to form a group that focused on pedagogy.

NSSE—Often pronounced "nessie," National Survey of Student Engagement, started with funding from the Pew Charitable Trusts and now funded through institutional participation fees and administered through the Indiana University Center for Survey Research. The survey is designed to get information from participating institutions about student participation in programs and activities—measuring how students spend their time and determining what they gain from college. A recent publication based on the surveys is *Student Success in College: Creating Conditions that Matter* (Kuh et al.). Not related to the National Society for the Study of Education, also abbreviated NSSE.

Ombuds Office—The office charged with conflict management, dispute resolution, and problem-solving in a fair and impartial manner. Complaints may be made in confidence to the Ombuds person about conduct or conflicts that arise in the workplace, and can come from students, faculty, administrators, or staff.

Portland Resolution—A document developed by the Council of Writing Program Administrators to describe the working conditions necessary for being an effective WPA and outline conditions for equitable treatment of WPAs in the evaluation process, especially with regard to tenure and promotion. It came out of the 1990 meeting of the Council of Writing Program Administrators in Portland, OR.

Program assessment—Assessment of a program or department, required as a part of the accreditation process; the Council of Writing Program Administrators offers a Consultant-Evaluator service to assess writing programs separately from other program assessments (of the English department, for example). The AAC & U Website has a helpful glossary of assessment terms, from the Spring 2002 issue of their publication *Peer Review:* www.aacu.org/peerreview/pr.sp02reality.cfm.

RCB/RCM—Responsibility Centered Budget/Management. A decentralized budgeting system that puts the deans in charge of resources but also, in many cases, requires that they pay for all services from other units. In some forms, this budgeting system distributes resources according to enrollments.

SAT—First known as Scholastic Achievement Test (when it was first given in 1926), then Scholastic Aptitude Test, then Scholastic Assessment Test, now simply SAT. Originally developed to ensure that students of merit, not simply students of privilege, had access to higher education, these standardized tests have come increasingly under fire by those who see them as exclusionary, discriminating against under-represented groups. Some institutions are not requiring the SAT for admissions as a result. The SAT reasoning test (formerly SAT I), includes mathematics, critical reasoning, and writing; it is all multiple-choice except for a 25-minute essay, scored holistically; this new version of the test has also come under criticism, especially by Les Perelman of MIT, who found a high correlation between the length of the essay and a high score.

SCH—Student credit hour, a unit of measure that represents 50 minutes of instruction. Courses meet three times a week over a 15-week semester or four or five times a week over a 12- or 10-week quarter; the credit hours earned are applied to the number of total hours a student needs to graduate. Budgets in some institutions are figured on number of student credit hours generated per department.

Shared governance—A form of institutional governance that, in its ideal state, allows matters of policy and procedure (with regard to, for example, curricula or personnel) to be decided jointly between faculty and the administration.

Soft money—Money that cannot be depended upon to be always available (such as a pledge not yet donated or money temporarily coming from grant support).

Strategic plan—An administrative initiative to determine the long-range goals of the institution, given its mission. These are usually five-year plans, but can be longer. Budget requests are sometimes required to be tied to the strategic plan.

Temporary dollars—Funding, usually for non-tenure-track temporary faculty appointments, that is generated from open lines (faculty who have retired), sabbaticals, leaves without pay, etc.

Unit—A budgetary unit, such as a department, program, or center.

Unrestricted funds—Money that can be used without restrictions (for food and alcohol, for example), usually from donations.

6 Practical Resources for Writing Program Administrators: A Selected Bibliography

Anne Whitney

General Resource Guides/Overviews

Adler-Kassner, Linda, and Gregory R. Glau. *The Bedford Bibliography for Teachers of Basic Writing.* 2nd Ed. New York: Bedford/St. Martin's, 2005. (Available online at http://www.bedfordstartins.com/basicbib/)

Reynolds, Nedra, Bruce Herzberg, and Patricia Bizzell. *The Bedford Bibliography for Teachers of Writing.* 6th Ed. New York: Bedford/St. Martin's, 2003. (Available online at <http://www.bedfordstmartins.com/bb/>.)

These two comprehensive annotated bibliographies are available free of charge online and are resources for both the new teacher of composition as well as the new or experienced WPA needing a quick reference. Sections in *The Bedford Bibliography for Teachers of Writing* include "Resources," "History and Theory," "Composing, Literacy, and the Rhetorics of Writing," "Curriculum Development," and "Writing Programs." Sections in *The Bedford Bibliography for Teachers of Basic Writing* include "History and Theory: Basic Writing and Basic Writers," "Pedagogical Issues," "Curriculum Development," and "An Administrative Focus."

Brown, Stuart C., Theresa Enos, and Catherine Chaput. *The Writing Program Administrator's Resource: A Guide to Reflective Institutional Practice.* Mahwah, NJ: Lawrence Erlbaum Associates, 2002.

Divided into two broad sections, "Instituting Change" and "Instituting Practice," this handbook is a collection of essays from established authorities in the field addressing problems and issues both local and global. The first section, "Instituting Change," discusses WPA work as it is situated within the college or university and within the wider landscape of academia; chapters address, for example, "Politics and the WPA" (Douglas D. Hesse), "Certifying the Knowledge of WPAs" (Gail Stygall), "Teaching a Graduate Course in Writing Program Administration" (Edward M. White), "Moving Up the Administrative Ladder" (Susan H. McLeod), and "Part-Time/Adjunct Issues: Working Toward Change" (Eileen E. Schell). The second section, "Instituting Practice," addresses the myriad practical problems WPAs experience, offering suggestions for action but also reflections on and thoughtful rationales for recommended practices. Topics include, for example, "Figuring it Out: Writing Programs in the Context of University Budgets" (Chris M. Anson), "Hard Work and Hard Data: Using Statistics to Help Your Program" (Gregory R. Glau), "Writing Program Administration and Instructional Computing" (Ken S. McAllister and Cynthia L. Selfe). The volume also includes an excellent annotated bibliography.

Council of Writing Program Administrators: http://wpacouncil.org.

The Council of Writing Program Administrators is the primary professional organization for WPAs. Its resources, all available through its website, include the refereed journal *WPA: Writing Program Administration,* online discussion forums, an annual conference, and a consultant-evaluator service for writing programs.

Janangelo, Joseph, and Kristine Hansen, Eds. *Resituating Writing: Constructing and Administering Writing Programs.* Crosscurrents: New Perspectives in Rhetoric and Composition. Portsmouth, NH: Boynton/Cook, 1995.

These essays on writing program administration go beyond practical guidelines to constitute scholarship in the field. The pieces articulate theory and raise a scholarly agenda along with a political one: "We want to resituate writing programs in the academy—not just physically [. . .] but conceptually as well—to take them from the margins and locate them at the center of undergraduate education. We hope to take them out of the purely service category they have occupied for so long and permit them to take their place with other respected units in the academy" (xvi). Indeed, several of the essays collected here, written by experienced WPAs, have since become classic pieces, cited often.

Rose, Shirley K, and Irwin Weiser, Eds. *The Writing Program Administrator as Researcher: Inquiry in Action & Reflection.* Portsmouth, NH: Boynton/Cook Publishers, 1999.

The essays in *The WPA as Researcher* combine descriptions of specific research activities engaged in by WPAs (Part I) with a general discussion of issues relevant to WPA researchers such as methods (historical, archival, postmodern mapping) and politics (Part II). The volume reflects the increasing understanding among WPAs and in composition generally that WPA work is not only compatible with research but is inextricably enmeshed with it.

Rose, Shirley K, and Irwin Weiser, Eds. *The Writing Program Administrator as Theorist.* Portsmouth, NH: Boynton/Cook/Heinemann, 2002.

The essays in this collection address the notion that WPA work is in fact theoretical work: WPAs draw upon, develop, and refine theory in their practice. The book's two parts correspond with the two major contexts in which WPAs work: the context of the individual institutions in which WPAs work (Part I) and the context of the field (Part II). Chapters include both discussions of WPA theorizing considered broadly and discussions of specific projects that could serve as models for scholarship.

Ward, Irene, and William J. Carpenter. *The Allyn & Bacon Sourcebook for Writing Program Administrators.* 1st ed. New York: Longman, 2002.

This text is a practical, how-to compendium for WPAs, containing eleven original articles and many more reprinted from *WPA: Writing Program Administration, ADE Bulletin,* and *College English.* The first two sections, "Who Are You as an Administrator?" and "Administering, Managing, Leading," are especially appropriate for the new administrator, providing basic orientations to that role. Part III, "Teaching Assistant Training and Staff Development" and Part IV, "Curriculum Design and Assessment," assemble and present major research in those two areas, providing a sensible starting point and set of rationales for the WPA designing policies and programs. The chapters in Part V discuss "Promotion and Professional Issues for WPAs," considering the WPA's situation as both faculty member and administrator.

WPA Listserv, Information and instructions available at http://wpacouncil.org/wpa-l

This e-mail discussion list is an international forum for writing program administrators at all kinds of institutions. Topics range from classroom strategies to institutional concerns.

Curriculum and Pedagogy

Association of Departments of English. "ADE Guidelines for Class Size and Workload for college and University Teachers of English: A Statement of Policy." 1992. Policy Statement. <http://www.ade.org/policy/policy_guidelines.htm>

NCTE College Section. "Statement on Class Size and Teacher Workload: College." 1987. Position Statement. <http://www.ncte.org/about/over/positions/category/class/107626.htm>.

Taken together, these two statements—the former from the Association of Departments of English (ADE), and the latter from the college section of the National Council of Teachers of English (NCTE)—present recommendations limiting class sizes and faculty student loads. This is the discipline's standard, helpful for making arguments to administrators accustomed to more traditional, large lecture-based models of classroom instruction.

"CCCC Position Statement on Teaching, Learning, and Assessing Writing in Digital Environments." NCTE. 2004. Position Statement. <http://www.ncte.org/cccc/resources/positions/123773.htm>.

This position statement presents recommendations for best practice in using technology in writing instruction, including positions on online courses and on machine scoring of student writing.

Corbett, Edward P. J., Nancy Myers, and Gary Tate, eds. *The Writing Teacher's Sourcebook.* 4th ed. New York: Oxford UP, 2000.

The editors have collected articles from prominent voices in the teaching of composition in a volume meant to serve as a basic compendium. Its "General" section addresses the context for composition at the end of the twentieth century. The "Theory" section includes three clusters of articles presenting frameworks for understanding what composition is and rationales for composition pedagogies. Finally, the "Practice" section's six clusters of essays present teaching approaches and problems ranging from planning for instruction to such specifics as grammar and the paragraph. Each cluster is followed by a list of additional readings on the topics presented.

Ferris, Dana, and John S. Hedgecock. *Teaching ESL Composition: Purpose, Process, and Practice.* Mahwah, NJ: Lawrence Erlbaum Associates, 1998.

Ferris and Hedgecock's resource on teaching English learners combines (a) solid overviews of current theory, (b) clear, use-in-class-tomorrow examples of teaching activities, and (c) questions for reflection and discussion appropriate for use in a TA seminar or faculty study group. The volume covers the full range of issues pertinent to ESL instruction, ranging from the reading-writing connection to constructing assignments to grammar and correctness.

Hillocks, George, Jr. *Teaching Writing as Reflective Practice.* New York: Teachers College Press, 1995.

George Hillocks weaves together innumerable strands of theory and wide-ranging experiences in secondary school and college writing classrooms to present a unified view of what can work in teaching composition, why it works, and how to organize instruction so that it will have a chance to work. The resulting picture of composition teaching is a teaching that is reflective (Chapter 2); integrates theoretical, experiential, and research knowledge (Chapter 3) in a constructive-developmental framework (Chapter Four); considers the composing process in all its complexity and variability (Chapter 4); and centers on the areas of discourse and inquiry as essential knowledge for writers (Chapter 5). Hillocks illustrates this ambitious and comprehensive portrait with concrete examples of planning for instruction: setting goals (Chapter 7), developing "gateway activities" that move students beyond their initial competence levels (Chapter 8), sequencing classroom activities (Chapter 9), and, finally, working with students in the classroom, adjusting and refining plans upon reasoned reflection in the moment of instruction (Chapter 10). In the end, Hillocks presents an approach to teaching writing that makes both theoretical and practical sense, a richly detailed portrait of teaching as challenging, complex, and yet ultimately possible.

Palmquist, Michael, Kate Kiefer, James Hartvigsen, and Barbara Goodlew. *Transitions: Teaching Writing in Computer-Supported and Traditional Classrooms.* Greenwich, CT: Ablex, 1998.

These authors' goal is "to explore the contextual interactions between technology and writing instruction" (xiv). In particular, they examine the various transitions at hand as writing instruction increasingly makes use of computers through two studies: the Transitions Study followed four faculty members and their students as they taught essentially the same courses in both computer classrooms and traditional classrooms; the New Teachers Study followed three novice composition instructors learning to teach writing in computer classrooms. While the volume is primarily a presentation of research, it includes frequent sidebars that point out specific teaching strategies readers might use in their own transitions into teaching with computers.

Tate, Gary, Amy Rupiper, and Kurt Schick, eds. *A Guide to Composition Pedagogies.* New York: Oxford UP, 2001.

This collection of twelve essays provides an overview of the major pedagogical approaches currently in use in composition, resulting in an orientation guide for beginning instructors or those new to the field. Approaches addressed include process (Lad Tobin), expressive (Christopher Burnham), rhetorical (William A. Covino), collaborative (Rebecca Moore Howard), cultural studies (Diana George and John Trimbur), critical (Ann George), feminist (Susan C. Jarratt), community-service (Laura Julier), writing across the curriculum (Susan McLeod), writing centers (Eric H. Hobson), basic writing (Deborah Mutnick), and technology (Charles Moran). The chapters both present the authors' own experiences with the approach and point to major scholarship that someone interested in the approach would do well to read.

Assessment and Accountability

Angelo, Thomas A. and Cross, K. Patricia. *Classroom Assessment Techniques: A Handbook for College Teachers.* 2nd ed. San Francisco: Jossey-Bass, 1993.

This handbook is directed at college teachers across disciplines rather than at writing teachers in particular, and it thus at times reflects an orientation toward the large lecture kind of classroom. However, it is worth overlooking those sections, for the rest of the book is a resource for instructors who wish to use assessment not only for assigning grades (which is covered here) but for learning about students' thinking and growth and learning about their own teaching effectiveness. The book's Part One provides clear advice and multiple practical examples for setting teaching goals and setting out to assess progress towards those goals. Part Two describes and provides examples of specific techniques for assessing prior knowledge, recall, understanding, and skills as varied as analysis, synthesis, and problem-solving. Student attitudes and students' reactions to instruction are also addressed here. Finally, Part Three suggests how faculty can act on the insights gained from assessment to reflect and improve.

Broad, Bob. *What We Really Value: Beyond Rubrics in Teaching and Assessing Writing.* Logan: Utah State UP, 2003.

Broad's research at one university helps to clarify what rubrics can and cannot do for a writing program and its faculty. He reports on that institution's development and use of a non-rubric based assessment system he terms "Dynamic Criteria Mapping" (DCM), then explores its implications and makes recommendations for other universities to implement the system. In DCM, faculty gather to assess student portfolios without a rubric or scoring guide, instead working to make explicit those internal criteria that they already held before the session began and which presumably informed their classroom teaching.

Hamp-Lyons, Liz, and William Condon. *Assessing the Portfolio: Principles for Practice, Theory, and Research.* Cresskill, NJ: Hampton Press, 2000.

Hamp-Lyons and Condon make a case for large-scale portfolio assessment programs as an alternative to more traditional testing and timed-writing assessments. After discussing the history of portfolio assessment in general (Chapter 1), the volume establishes a clear theoretical and research context for their use: Chapter 2 provides a delineation of nine characteristics of portfolios (collection, range, context richness, delayed evaluation, selection, student-centered control, reflection and self-assessment, growth along specific parameters, and development over time), and then demonstrates how those features of portfolios can be employed within the context of a variety of theoretical approaches to composition. Particularly useful to WPAs are the authors' discussions of portfolio assessment in practice (Chapter 3) and of developing a sound theoretical approach to their implementation (Chapter 4). Finally, Chapter 5 proposes a research agenda for further inquiry.

Huot, Brian A. *(Re)articulating Writing Assessment for Teaching and Learning.* Logan: Utah State UP, 2002.

Huot seeks to redefine the terms of composition's discourse on assessment and to rearticulate—or in some cases articulate clearly for the first time—exactly what we mean when we say "assessment." He stresses the fundamental differences between types and purposes of assessment activities (such as grading, testing, and evaluating) and argues for a more clearly defined field inquiry in to assessment with an explicit focus on validity. He discusses teachers' response to student writing, arguing that what is most needed and most effective is an account of the teacher's response *as a reader*. He explores the connection between assessment and classroom teaching, and he demonstrates the sometimes unstated theoretical orientations that necessarily underlie all instances of writing assessment. Finally, he considers writing assessment as a form of research and provides two practical models of writing assessment.

Royer, Dan, and Roger Gilles, eds. *Directed Self-Placement: Principles and Practices.* Cresskill, NJ: Hampton Press, 2003.

The essays in this collection describe an alternative to the test scores, placement tests, and portfolio assessments most colleges use to place students in first-year writing courses. In DSP, students receive clear information about course expectations and advice on how to make a decision about which courses to take, and then students decide on their own placements. Chapters in this volume describe several universities' approaches to DSP and explore the issues it raises.

White, Edward M. *Assigning, Responding, Evaluating: A Writing Teacher's Guide.* 4th ed. New York: Bedford, Freeman, Worth, 2007.

This book is written for instructors as a guide to "developing worthwhile writing assignments, responding sensitively to what students write, and evaluating that work intelligently and fairly" (vii). The first chapter, "Writing Assignments and Essay Topics," is particularly appropriate for use with beginning instructors or TAs, as it encourages thoughtful and explicit framing of writing tasks for students and includes many concrete example assignments along with teaching and scoring tips; also helpful for new instructors is "Responding to and Grading Student Writing" (Chapter 6). The rest of the volume speaks more to testing than to classroom instruction (though White argues convincingly throughout that the two must inherently be linked in order for either to be useful): chapters include "Helping Students Do Well on Essay Tests," "Placement or Diagnostic Essay Tests Based on Personal Experience," "Placement or Diagnostic Essay Tests Based on Given Texts," "Exit and Proficiency Examinations," and "Using Portfolios: Definitions, Strengths, and Weaknesses."

Wolcott, Willa, and Sue M. Legg. *An Overview of Writing Assessment: Theory, Research, and Practice.* Urbana, IL.: NCTE, 1998.

While the authors' stated audience for this book is first and foremost individual teachers using assessment in individual classrooms, most of the discussion in fact focuses on large-scale assessments such as those used for placement or program evaluation. Each chapter then concludes with "tips for teachers" that illustrate how such assessments need not be sharply divorced from the regular life of the classroom. They define and provide specific examples of a range of assessment approaches (such as impromptu samples, multiple samples or portfolios) and scoring approaches (such as holistic, analytic, or primary trait). They advise readers on topic design and provide clear discussions of validity and reliability. An especially helpful chapter describes procedures for training scorers to maximize inter-rater reliability—an enlightening exercise for any writing program faculty even outside the context of a formal assessment. Final chapters address cross-curricular assessment issues, issues of equity in assessment, and the future of writing assessment.

Yancey, Kathleen Blake, and Irwin Weiser, eds. *Situating Portfolios: Four Perspectives.* Logan, UT: Utah State UP, 1997.

This collection of essays includes contributions from authorities across composition considering the impact and implications of the now-widespread use of portfolios. Essays in the first section, "Theory and Power," consider portfolios in a range of theoretical lights, describe a range of current portfolio applications, and point out problematic aspects of those applications. The second section, "Pedagogy," includes essays on the relationship between portfolios and the actual work that students and teachers do together in classrooms. In the third section, "Teaching and Professional Development," essays discuss teacher portfolios both as evaluation tools and as tools for reflection and growth. Finally, a "Technology" section takes up how technologies such as hypertext and digital media are changing—and not changing—portfolios.

Staffing and Staff Development

Dunn, Richard J. "Teaching Assistance, Not Teaching Assistants." *ADE Bulletin* 97 (1990): 47–50.

Dunn recommends reforms for the way teaching assistants' work is structured in order that PhD programs in English also work effectively as induction programs for new college faculty. Specifically, he recommends manageable workloads, integration between what graduate students in English are teaching and what they are learning, a progression from supervised, auxiliary roles to independent teaching, serious graduate courses in pedagogy, and TA participation in the life of the department, especially where curricular decisions are made.

Ebest, Sally Barr. *Changing the Way We Teach: Writing and Resistance in the Training of Teaching Assistants.* Carbondale, IL: Southern Illinois UP, 2005.

A resource for those WPAs who work with TAs, this book addresses the problem of resistance among graduate student writing instructors—why they so often resist instruction in TA preparation programs, the sources of that resistance, its implications for those TAs' classroom teaching, and, thankfully, ways of working with TAs to reduce resistance and encourage change. In a study of eighteen TAs over five years, Ebest found that engaging graduate students in writing activities—those same activities in which they might be expected to engage their own students—helped TAs into self-efficacy, reflection, and innovation as novice writing instructors.

Eble, Kenneth Eugene. *The Craft of Teaching: A Guide to Mastering the Professor's Art.* 2nd ed. San Francisco: Jossey-Bass, 1988.

Eble presents an orientation to college teaching in any discipline that is accessible to those who have previously not thought much about what makes good teaching beyond the ways they themselves were taught. He begins with a general overview of some issues that are important to teaching, such as the myths and assumptions the general population tends to hold and how those relate to what students actually need from and experience in college courses. The second part of the book describes modes of instruction, with chapters on classroom climate, lecture, discussion, mentoring, and student-directed learning. The book's third section addresses practical matters such as choosing and assigning texts, testing and grading, and handling classroom problems such as cheating. Finally, Eble turns his attention to the skills and habits of mind a teacher needs to *continue* improving as an instructor through lifelong professional development.

Good, Tina LaVonne, and Leanne B. Warshauer, eds. *In Our Own Voice: Graduate Students Teach Writing.* Boston: Allyn and Bacon, 2000.

This is a collection of essays written by and for teaching assistants teaching first-year composition. The selections address those issues TAs tend to find salient: the position of TAs within the university, the tension between challenging students to question their biases and assumptions and creating a safe space for students to take risks as writers, authority issues, the place of personal writing in a composition course, teaching grammar, and responding to student writing.

Hesse, Douglas. "Teachers as Students, Reflecting Resistance." *College Composition and Communication* 44 (1993): 224–31.

Hesse argues that when graduate student instructors read theory for their courses (such as reading composition theory in a seminar for new TAs), they find themselves in the same "beginner" positions as are students in the first-year composition courses those graduate students are teaching. Challenged and frustrated by new kinds of discourse in which they are not yet fully-fledged participants, they often resist engaging with the texts at all or dismiss the content thereof as "jargon" or simply "stupid." He describes his own approach to helping graduate students past this resistance, in turn illuminating how TAs might do the same for their students.

Hult, Christine A., ed. *Evaluating Teachers of Writing.* Urbana, IL: NCTE, 1994.

This collection of essays provides guidance for WPAs struggling to find fair and meaningful ways to evaluate writing program faculty. Part I provides a theoretical orientation to faculty evaluation. The essays in Part II cover specific evaluation methods, including peer reviews, student evaluations, and videotaped microteaching. Part III addresses issues particular to specific groups of faculty, such as adjuncts, TAs, or disciplinary faculty in WAC programs.

McKeachie, Wilbert J. and Marilla D. Svinicki. *McKeachie's Teaching Tips.* 12th ed. New York: Houghton Mifflin, 2006.

McKeachie's paperback has become a standard text for new college faculty, but it might also be appropriate for experienced instructors who are ready to experiment. The first section includes a chapter on planning a course, walking the reader through the three months prior to a course (including such practical matters as choosing texts and designing a syllabus) and the first day of class (including icebreakers and ways of orienting the course around those concerns the professor feels are most important). A second section covers basic classroom activities such as facilitating discussion, lecturing, assessment, and grading, including plenty of specific examples and advice. In the third section, chapters reflect on the issues and needs that students bring to the classroom, including motivation and problems that can arise in the teacher-student relationship. The fourth, fifth, and sixth sections address a comprehensive range of strategies and skills for student-centered, active learning, varying from setting up collaborative and problem-based activities, to facilitating practical and lab experiences for students, to fostering critical thinking and independence in students. The book closes with advice on the faculty member as a growing, learning professional throughout one's career.

Nyquist, Jody D., ed. *Preparing the Professoriate of Tomorrow to Teach: Selected Readings in TA Training.* Dubuque, IA: Kendall/Hunt, 1991.

This collection of essays addressing TA training across disciplines considers the role of TAs in the university-at-large and offers practical suggestions for preparing them to teach. Section 3 in particular describes university-wide TA training programs, and Section IV presents specific activities and strategies to use in training sessions. See especially the following composition-specific chapters: Gottschalk,

"Training TAs Across the Curriculum to Teach Writing: Embracing Diversity" (Chapter 21); Back, Carlton, Wolk, and Schulze, "Training TAs to Teach Writing: Four Perspectives on Creating a Community for Composition Instruction" (Chapter 25); and Berson, "Great Expectations: Setting Achievable Goals in English Composition" (Chapter 36). In addition, Section V presents advice for WPAs in their role as supervisors of TAs.

"Statement on Non-Tenure-Track Faculty Members." *MLA.* 2003. <http://www.mla.org/statement_on_nonten>.

"Statement from the Conference on the Growing Use of Part-Time and Adjunct Faculty." *NCTE.* 1997. <http://www.ncte.org/about/over/positions/category/profcon/107662.htm>.

Taken together, these two documents provide practical and ethical guidelines for the use of part-time and non-tenure track faculty, as has traditionally been common in composition and which, under budgetary pressure, tends to become even more so. These are useful both for setting policy within a writing program and for arguing for that policy to university administrators.

Strenski, Ellen. "Helping TAs across the Curriculum Teach Writing: An Additional Use for the TA Handbook." *WPA: Writing Program Administration* 15.3 (1992): 68–73.

Strenski recommends that WPAs contribute a section to the university's campus-wide teaching assistant handbook that suggests some of the best practices now common in composition classrooms. These include, for example, asking students to write in class, organizing peer review sessions, or establishing clear evaluation criteria before students write. Contributing thus to the campus' TA handbook would support beginning instructors and would help contribute to writing across the curriculum efforts across the institution.

Administrative and Professional Issues

Boyer, Ernest L. *Scholarship Reconsidered: Priorities of the Professoriate.* Princeton, NJ: Carnegie Foundation for the Advancement of Teaching, 1990.

This now-classic text proposes a framework for faculty evaluation that takes into account modes of scholarship beyond the narrow definition of research that has been exclusively prioritized in the American university since WWII. He presents a scheme incorporating "the scholarship of discovery" (most like basic research), "the scholarship of integration" (interdisciplinary and interpretive work), "the scholarship of application" (service tied to one's field of knowledge), and "the scholarship of teaching." Many universities have since taken up this framework in efforts to reform faculty advancement procedures.

"Scholarship in Composition: Guidelines for Faculty, Deans, and Department Chairs." *NCTE.* 1987. <http://www.ncte.org/about/over/positions/category/write/107681.htm>.

This statement "describing the range of scholarly activity in composition" serves as a guide for evaluating composition faculty's scholarship for purposes of tenure and promotion. This meets a need in many English departments, where the members of review committees may be literature scholars unsure how to evaluate the unfamiliar models of scholarship (such as those based in the social sciences) prevalent in composition.

"Evaluating the Intellectual Work of Writing Administration.". *Council of Writing Program Administrators.* 1998 <http://wpacouncil.org/positions/intellectualwork.html>.

Adopted by the Council of Writing Program Administrators in 1998, this document sets standards for how WPA work might be documented by WPAs for tenure and promotion purposes and how that work might be understood by university departments.

Gebhardt, Richard C., and Barbara Genelle Smith Gebhardt, eds. *Academic Advancement in Composition Studies: Scholarship, Publication, Promotion, Tenure.* Mahwah, NJ: Erlbaum, 1997. (Available online at <http://www.questia.com/PM.qst?a=o&se=ggl&docId=10111146>.)

This edited volume focuses on issues surrounding the status of work in composition studies as "scholarship" from the perspective of universities and departments. Chapters outline the history of thinking about the academic work of composition (R. Gebhardt), compare models of scholarship in composition and its frequent neighbor field, literature (Schilb), consider nonacademic publishing (Hesse and B. Gebhardt) and WPA work (Roen) as scholarship, and discuss the special situations of faculty at two-year colleges (Kroll and Alford), faculty in professional communication (Blyler, Graham, and Thralls), teachers of ESL and basic writing (Lay), and writing centers (Harris). Several chapters discuss personnel reviews in particular: after general advice (R. Gebhardt), chapters address the situation of women (Neulieb), mentoring (Enos; R. Gebhardt), and external reviews (Bloom). A final chapter considers faculty reviews from a dean's point of view (McLeod).

Goonen, Norma M., and Rachel S. Blechman. *Higher Education Administration: A Guide to Legal, Ethical, and Practical Issues.* The Greenwood Educators' Reference Collection. Westport, CN.: Greenwood Press, 1999.

Goonen and Blechman strike a balance between describing legal obligations, discussing ethical complexities, and making clear practical suggestions for administrators. Chapters address the hiring process, issues of compensation and continuing employment, tenure and promotion, terminating employees, academic freedom, disputes with students, and academic records. The volume provides a survey of potential problems and guidelines for navigating them.

Hult, Christine A. et al. "'The Portland Resolution': Guidelines for Writing Program Administrator Positions." *WPA: Writing Program Administration* 16.1–2 (1992): 88–94. (Available online at <http://wpacouncil.org/positions/portlandres.html>.)

This document outlines the role of a WPA, detailing appropriate responsibilities, qualifications, and workload. The guidelines constitute a set of professional standards, articulated by members of the profession themselves, for the characteristics of high quality WPA work; they also guard against unworkable job descriptions for WPAs or the appointment of unqualified persons to WPA roles.

Kinkead, Joyce, and Jeanne Simpson. "The Administrative Audience: A Rhetorical Problem." *WPA: Writing Program Administration* 23.3 (2000): 68-77.

Former WPAs who have since become central university administrators reflect on the misconceptions they held about central administration when they were directing writing programs and make recommendations for WPAs. They present a primer on administrative culture and terms and describe ways of preparing proposals that sensitive to the administrator as reader.

MLA Commission on Professional Service. "Making Faculty Work Visible: Reinterpreting Professional Service, Teaching, and Research in the Fields of Language and Literature." *MLA*. 1996. <http://www.mla.org/pdf/profserv96.pdf>.

This document, which is the report from an MLA commission examining the "Professional service" leg of the familiar triad "Research, Teaching, and Service," describes a number of service roles enacted by English and composition faculty and makes recommendations about how that work might be considered for the purposes of academic advancement.

Myers-Breslin, Linda, ed. *Administrative Problem-Solving for Writing Programs and Writing Centers: Scenarios in Effective Program Management*. Urbana, IL: NCTE, 1999.

This collection provides a series of case studies and example scenarios that illustrate administrative problems WPAs are likely to face and ways of solving those problems. The scenarios are organized into three categories: "Selection and Training" includes, for instance, hiring and training TAs or staffing a writing center. "Program Development" includes, for example, developing WAC programs, funding a writing center, or integrating technology. Perhaps most helpful to new WPAs, "Professional Issues of Departmental Authority and Professional Development" addresses such concerns as introducing change in a less than enthusiastic environment, thinking about the physical space a program occupies, or managing a relationship with a writing center.

Notes

Notes to Chapter 2

[1] Although there has been some improvement since the advent of affirmative action, academe is still very male-dominated. Sally Barr-Ebest surveyed WPAs in 1992 and reported her findings in "Gender Differences in Writing Administration"; she found that despite their common training, duties, and responsibilities, men fared better as WPAs than did women: they were paid more, they published more, and they were more likely to get tenure.

[2] The preview issue was bound as a double issue with *New York Magazine*.

[3] The resolution was first drafted at a conference of the Council of Writing Program Administrators held in Portland, OR.

[4] Like the Portland Resolution, this position statement has not been without its critics. See Schneider and Marback.

Notes to Chapter 3

[1] In the past decade a few required writing courses have appeared in Canada and in parts of Europe, especially the Netherlands.

[2] Harvard was established by the Puritans of the Massachusetts Bay Colony, William and Mary by the Anglicans, Princeton by the Presbyterians, Brown (then the College of Rhode Island) by Baptists, Rutgers (then Queen's College) by the Dutch Reformed Church, and Dartmouth by the Congregationalists (see Spring 61–62).

[3] Although the "common school" movement of the 1830s and 40s had begun to establish the basis for the present American public school system, very few students attended what we now think of as high school in any form (see Spring Chapter 4). It wasn't until a landmark decision by the Michigan Supreme Court in 1874 that school districts were required to maintain tax-supported high schools (Spring 195–96).

[4] Wallace Douglas argues that the Statute of the Boylston Professorship was an essential factor in the origins of Freshman composition in "Rhetoric for the Meritocracy." It is interesting to speculate about Hill's journalistic

career as one of the reasons for the focus on correctness in Harvard's composition courses.

[5] Donald Stewart discusses the dominant influence of Harvard men in the early years of the Modern Language Association in "Harvard's Influence on English Studies," and what he calls the "Harvardization" of English in "Two Model Teachers and the Harvardization of English Departments." In his discussion of the teaching of writing during this period, however, S. Michael Halloran argues that the influence of Harvard on English studies has been exaggerated (" From Rhetoric to Composition").

[6] Hill's 1895 *Rhetoric* began with a section on grammatical purity, followed by a section on words and word choice, a section on arrangement that focused on clearness, force, and ease, and a final section on kinds of compositions: description, narration, exposition, and argument.

[7] Brereton objects to the term "current-traditional," stating that such a term "by its very nature lumps together a vast array of practices in the interest of making a larger point. And it discourages us from looking at a whole range of educational practices that were occurring in those supposedly weak composition courses that proliferated for nearly a century. In other words, interpreting the history of composition as a loss and then a revival of rhetoric has given a partial view, a view that explicitly devalues almost a century of teaching and learning" (*Origins* xiii). Nevertheless, the term provides a useful shorthand for a model of composition instruction that assumed a deficit model of student writing, one that was widespread up until the 1970s.

[8] JoAnn Campbell discusses the effects of rising enrollments on the workload of faculty at Vassar during Gertrude Buck's time there, 1897–1920, in "Women's Work." Susan Miller, in an examination of selected university catalogs over the period from 1920 to 1960, documents the fact that the teaching faculty in English Departments doubled over that period [67]; although the ranks of the faculty were growing, that growth was not keeping pace with rising enrollments. She lists the catalogs she examined as follows: "Arizona, Berkeley, Colorado, Cornell, Georgia, Harvard, Iowa, Kansas, Michigan, Nebraska, North Carolina, Oregon, Stanford, Washington, and Wisconsin-Madison" (67).

[9] There is an odd twentieth century parallel in the history of Michigan's English Composition Board (ECB), one of the oldest writing across the curriculum programs in the country. For reasons similar to the demise of the Rhetoric Department, as well as for budgetary reasons, the ECB also disappeared as an independent unit. See McLeod, "WAC at Century's End: Haunted by the Ghost of Fred Newton Scott."

[10] Winifred Bryan Horner notes this fact, including herself among the group of early WPAs trained in English Education as well as Edward Corbett, James Kinneavy, C. Jan Swearingen, and Frank D'Angelo (Ramey and Takayoshi "Watson Conference Oral History #4").

[11] Like many early WPAs who were strong personalities, Baird's influence extended beyond Amherst; Ann Berthoff referred to those who were influenced by English 1–2 and who then went elsewhere to teach as the "Amherst Mafia" (72). Varnum includes Walker Gibson and William Coles, among others, in the list of those influenced by the course. John Brereton, in a discussion of his own history as a scholar-teacher, states that as a graduate student learning to teach writing at Rutgers, he was led by people who had gone through the Amherst program and who passed on many of the principles of that program to them: an extremely close examination of text, "intense concentration on the exact wording of assignments," a close link between one assignment and the next, and a breaking down of assignments into careful steps, leading up to the actual writing assignment, often couched as an invitation ("Symposium"495). Brereton states that there are still traces of this Amherst-to-Rutgers heritage in linked assignments and carefully wrought assignments in the work of David Bartholomae, Don McQuade, Bob Atwan, Linda Flower, Patricia Bizzell, and Bruce Herzberg, all of whom were in the Rutgers graduate program in literature during the late 1960s and early 1970s (495).

[12] There were in fact eight sessions sponsored by the Teaching of Writing Division that year (nine counting the cash bar), as listed on p. 986 of the conference program: #9 (Plenary Session), #139 (Training and Retraining Writing Teachers), #212 (Writing and Reading), #384 (Measurement of Growth and Proficiency in Writing), #415 (Research in Teaching Writing), #448 (Writing Program Administration), #538 (Applied Linguistics and the Teaching of Writing), and #637 (Organizational Meeting).

[13] Some members of CCCC who remembered the early days of the organization were none too happy about the formation of this new organization. Richard Lloyd-Jones recalls that in the mid-1970s CCCC was not sure of its own life—after large conferences in the 1960s, the meeting at Anaheim in 1974 had fewer than 600 attendees. "As civil rights issues grew and more and more of the comp people came from two year colleges (which did not encourage professional memberships), CCCC was pressed[. . .]. Some CCCCers saw WPA as taking away their reason for being. I'd say that CCCC had already abdicated that basis, but didn't realize it." (e-mail).

[14] The title of the Portland Resolution was meant to echo that of the Wyoming Resolution, a grass-roots attempt to address the low professional status of composition teachers that was endorsed by the Executive Committee of CCCC at the Business meeting of the 1987 Conference (see Robertson et al. and the report from the CCCC Committee on Professional Standards for Quality Education). Although the Portland Resolution was almost universally hailed as a document that helped to define the work of the WPA, it was not without its critics. Gunner argues that the job of the WPA is "fundamentally and necessarily a political one; the job is not to administer,

effectively or otherwise, the courses whose object is the production of the conformist citizen" ("Politicizing the Portland Resolution" 29).

Notes to Chapter 4

[1] Further, they found that most first-year writing curricula seem to be textbook-driven. The majority of textbooks used by the respondents were readers, rather than rhetorics or handbooks; in half the cases teachers were required to use a particular book. The fact that most curricula are textbook-dependent is, of course, directly related to the fact that most writing courses are taught by TAs or contingent faculty, some of the latter hired at the last minute (and many of them with literature rather than composition training); a common textbook is then a convenient way of assuring truth in advertising—that all sections of a multi-section course, no matter who the teacher is, are at least using the same book. It is also a way of establishing consistency over time because there are new TAs and faculty coming in every year. Establishing the curriculum for the course often comes down to deciding which textbook(s) to use, and fortunately, there are now a number of such texts written and field-tested by experienced WPAs that can be used in shaping a curriculum.

[2] Sometimes this course is offered for university credit, and sometimes not, depending on local contexts and histories.

[3] There are also essays on writing center pedagogy (Eric H. Hobson) and the pedagogy of writing across the curriculum (Susan McLeod), which are somewhat tangential to the present discussion. There is a chapter entitled "Rhetorical Pedagogy" (William A. Covino) which I did not include; as Richard Fulkerson says, it is "mis-named and ill-fitted to the volume" since it focuses only on history and theory ("Composition at the Turn of the Twenty-First Century" 672).

Works Cited

"ADE Guidelines for Class Size and Workload for college and University Teachers of English: A Statement of Policy." Association of Departments of English. 11 November 2005. <http://www.ade.org/policy/policy_guidelines.htm>

Adler-Kassner, Linda, and Gregory Glau, eds. *The Bedford Bibliography for Teachers of Basic Writing*, 2nd ed. New York: Bedford/St. Martin's, 2005. 5 December 2006 <http://www.bedfordstmartins.com/basicbib>.

American Association of Community Colleges. 2006. 11 November. 2006. <http://www.aacc.nche.edu/Content/NavigationMenu/AboutCommunityColleges/HistoricalInformation/Historical_Information.htm>.

Amorose, Thomas. "WPA Work at the Small College or University: Reimagining Power and Making the Small School Visible." *WPA: Writing Program Administration* 23.3 (Spring 2000): 85–103.

Angelo, Thomas A. and Cross, K. Patricia. *Classroom Assessment Techniques: A Handbook for College Teachers.* 2nd ed. San Francisco: Jossey-Bass, 1993

Anson, Chris M. "Figuring It Out: Writing Programs in the Context of University Budgets." *The Writing Program Administrator's Resource: A Guide to Reflective Institutional Practice.* Ed. Stuart C. Brown and Theresa Enos. Mahwah, NJ: Erlbaum, 2002. 233–52.

Astin, Helen and Carole Leland. *Woman of Influence, Women of Vision: A Cross-Generational Study of Leaders and Social Change.* San Francisco: Jossey-Bass, 1991.

Aydelotte, Frank. *College English.* New York: Oxford UP, 1913.

Bain, Alexander. *English Composition and Rhetoric.* New York: D. Appleton, 1866.

Barr-Ebest, Sally. "Gender Differences in Writing Program Administration." *WPA: Writing Program Administration* 18.3 (Spring 1995): 53–73.

Bartholomae, David. "Freshman English, Composition, and CCCC." *College Composition and Communication* 40 (February 1989): 38–50.

Bartholomae, David, and Anthony Petrosky. *Facts, Artifacts and Counterfacts: Theory and Method for a Reading and Writing Course.* Upper Montclair, NJ: Boynton/Cook, 1986.

Bazerman, Charles. "Looking at Writing; Writing What I See." *Living Rhetoric and Composition: Stories of the Discipline*. Ed. Duane Roen, Stuart C. Brown, and Theresa Enos. Mahwah, NJ: Erlbaum. 1999. 15–24.
Belanoff, Pat, and Marcia Dickson. *Portfolios: Process and Product*. Portsmouth, NH: Boynton/Cook, 1991.
Belanoff, Pat, and Peter Elbow, eds. "Using Portfolios to Increase Collaboration and Community in a Writing Program." *WPA: Writing Program Administration* 9.3 (1986): 27–40.
Belcher, Diane, and Alan Hirvela, eds. *Linking Literacies: Perspectives on L2 Reading-Writing Connections*. Ann Arbor: U of Michigan P, 2004.
Berlin, James A. *Rhetoric and Reality: Writing Instruction in American Colleges 1900–1985*. Carbondale, IL: Southern Illinois UP: 1987.
—. *Writing Instruction in Nineteenth-Century American Colleges*. Carbondale, IL: Southern Illinois UP, 1984.
Berthoff, Ann E. "I.A. Richards." *Traditions of Inquiry*. Ed. John Brereton. New York: Oxford UP, 1985. 50–80.
Birnbaum, Robert. *How Colleges Work: the Cybernetics of Academic Organization and Leadership*. San Francisco: Jossey-Bass, 1988.
Bishop, Wendy. "Toward a Definition of a Writing Program Administrator: Expanding Roles and Evolving Responsibilities." *Freshman English News* 16.2 (Fall 1987): 11–14.
Bishop, Wendy, and Gay Lynn Crossley. "Doing the Hokey Pokey: Why Writing Program Administrators' Job Conditions Don't Seem to Be Improving." *Composition Studies/Freshman English News* 21.2 (1993): 46–59.
Bizzell, Patricia. "Foreward: On Good Administrators." *Kitchen Cooks, Plate Twirlers and Troubadours: Writing Program Administrators Tell Their Stories*. Ed. Diana George. Portsmouth, NH: Boynton/Cook Heinemann, 1999. vii-ix.
Black, Laurel, Donald A. Daiker, Jeffrey Sommers, and Gail Stygall, eds. *New Directions in Portfolio Assessment: Reflective Practice, Critical Theory, and Large-Scale Scoring*. Portsmouth, NH: Boynton/Cook, 1994.
Blanchard, Frances. *Frank Aydelotte of Swarthmore*. Middletown, CT: Wesleyan UP, 1970.
Bloom, Lynn Z. "I Want A Writing Director." *College Composition and Communication* 43.2 (1992): 176–78.
Bloom, Lynn Z., Donald Daiker, and Edward M. White, eds. *Composition Studies in the New Millennium: Rereading the Past, Rewriting the Future*. Carbondale, IL: Southern Illinois UP, 2003.
Bloom, Lynn Z., and Richard C. Gebhardt. "Coming of Age: The WPA Summer Workshops and Conference." *WPA: Writing Program Administration* 10.3 (Spring 1987): 53–57.

Bordelon, Suzanne. "The 'Advance' Toward Democratic Administration: Laura Johnson Wylie and Gertrude Buck of Vassar College." *Historical Studies of Writing Program Administration: Individuals, Communities, and the Formation of a Discipline.* Ed. Barbara L'Eplattenier and Lisa Mastrangelo. West Lafayette, IN: Parlor P, 2004. 91–115.

Born, Margaret. *The Jossey-Bass Academic Administrator's Guide to Budget and Financial Management.* San Francisco: Jossey-Bass, 2002.

Bousquet, Marc. "Composition as a Management Science: Toward a University Without a WPA." *JAC* 22.3 (2002): 493–526.

Bousquet, Marc, Tony Scott, and Leo Parascondola, eds. *Tenured Bosses and Disposable Teachers: Writing Instruction in the Managed University.* Carbondale, IL: Southern Illinois UP, 2004.

Boyer, Ernest. *Scholarship Reconsidered: Priorities of the Professoriate.* Princeton, NJ: Carnegie Foundation for the Advancement of Teaching, 1990.

Braddock, Richard Reed, Richard Lloyd-Jones, and Lowell Schoer. *Research in Written Composition.* Urbana, IL: NCTE, 1963.

Brereton, John, ed. *The Origins of Composition Studies in the American College, 1875–1925: A Documentary History.* Pittsburgh: U of Pittsburgh P, 1995.

—. "Symposium: Scholar, Teacher, WPA, Mentor." *College Composition and Communication* 56 (February 2005): 493–501.

Broad, Bob. *What We Really Value: Beyond Rubrics in Teaching and Assessing Writing.* Logan: Utah State UP, 2003.

Brown, Rollo Walter. *Dean Briggs.* New York: Harper, 1926.

Brown, Stuart C. "Applying Ethics: A Decision-Making Heuristic for Writing Program Administrators." *The Writing Program Administrator's Resource: A Guide to Reflective Institutional Practice.* Ed. Stuart C. Brown and Theresa Enos. Mahwah, NJ: Erlbaum, 2002. 155–63.

Brown, Stuart C., and Theresa Enos, eds. *The Writing Program Administrator's Resource: A Guide to Reflective Institutional Practice.* Mahwah, NJ: Erlbaum, 2002.

Bruffee, Kenneth. "The WPA as (Journal) Writer: What the Record Reveals." *WPA: Writing Program Administration* 9 (1985): 5–10.

—. "WPA at MLA." E-mail to the author. 3 June 2005.

Buck, Gertrude, and Elizabeth Woodbridge. *A Course in Expository Writing.* New York: Holt, 1899.

Bullock, Richard. "When Administration Becomes Scholarship: The Future of Writing Program Administration." *WPA: Writing Program Administration* 11 (Fall 1987): 13–18.

Bushman, Donald. "The WPA as Pragmatist: Recasting 'Service' as 'Human Science.' " *WPA: Writing Program Administration* 23.1–2 (Fall/Winter 1999): 29–43.

Butts, R. Freeman, and Lawrence A. Cremin. *History of Education in American Culture.* New York: Holt, 1953.
Cambridge, Barbara L., ed. *Electronic Portfolios: Emerging Practices in Student, Faculty, and Institutional Learning.* Washington, D.C.: American Association of Higher Education, 2001.
Cambridge, Barbara L., and Ben W. McClelland. "From Icon to Partner: Repositioning the Writing Program Administrator." *Resituating Writing: Constructing and Administering Writing Programs.* Ed. Joseph Janangelo and Kristine Hansen. Portsmouth, NH: Boynton/Cook Heinemann, 1995. 151–59.
Campbell, JoAnn. "Controlling Voices: The Legacy of English A at Radcliffe College 1883–1917." *College Composition and Communication* 43.4 (December 1992): 472–85.
—. *Toward a Feminist Rhetoric: The Writing of Gertrude Buck.* Pittsburgh: U of Pittsburgh P, 1996.
—. "Women's Work, Worthy Work: Composition Instruction at Vassar College, 1897–1992." *Constructing Rhetorical Education.* Ed. Marie Secor and Davida Charney. Carbondale, IL: Southern Illinois UP, 1992. 26–42.
Carpenter, William J. "Professional Development for Writing Program Staff." Ward and Carpenter, 156–65.
Carr, Jean Ferguson, Stephen L. Carr, and Lucille M. Schultz. *Archives of Instruction: Nineteenth-Century Rhetorics, Readers, and Composition Books in the United States.* Carbondale, IL: Southern Illinois UP, 2005.
Catalano, Timothy, et al. "TA Training in English: An Annotated Bibliography." *WPA: Writing Program Administration* 19.3 (Spring 1996): 36–54. Rpt. in Ward and Carpenter, 166–81.
CCCC Committee on Professional Standards for Quality Education. "CCCC Initiatives on the Wyoming Conference Resolution: A Draft Report." *College Composition and Communication* 40 (1989): 61–72.
CCCC Committee on Teaching, Learning, and Assessing Writing in Digital Environments. "Position Statement on Teaching, Learning, and Assessing Writing in Digital Environments." *College Composition and Communication* 55.4 (June 2004): 785–89.
CCCC Executive Committee. "Statement of Principles and Standards for the Postsecondary Teaching of Writing." *College Composition and Communication* 40 (October 1989): 329–36.
Chapman, David W., and Gary Tate. "A Survey of Doctoral Programs in Rhetoric and Composition." *Rhetoric Review* 5 (1987): 124–86.
Cheramie, Deany M. "Sifting Through Fifty Years of Change: Writing Program Administration at an Historically Black University." *Historical Studies of Writing Program Administration: Individuals, Communities, and the Formation of a Discipline.* Ed. Barbara L'Eplattenier and Lisa Mastrangelo. West Lafayette, IN: Parlor P, 2004. 145–65.

Clark, Irene, ed. *Concepts in Composition*. Mahwah, NJ: Erlbaum, 2002.
Connors, Robert J. *Composition-Rhetoric: Backgrounds, Theory, and Pedagogy*. Pittsburgh: U of Pittsburgh P, 1997.
—. "Composition History and Disciplinarity." *History, Reflection, and Narrative: The Professionalization of Composition, 1963–1983*. Ed. Mary Rosner, Beth Boem, and Debra Journet. Stamford, CT: Ablex, 1999. 3–21.
—. "Dreams and Play: Historical Method and Methodology." *Methods and Methodology in Composition Research*. Ed. Gesa Kirsch and Patricia A. Sullivan. Carbondale, IL: Southern Illinois UP, 1992. 15–36.
—. "Historical Inquiry in Composition Studies." *The Writing Instructor* 3 (1984): 157–67.
—. "Rhetoric in the Modern University: The Creation of an Underclass." *The Politics of Writing Instruction: Postsecondary*. Ed. Richard Bullock and John Trimbur. Portsmouth, NH: Boynton/Cook Heinemann, 1991. 55–84.
—. "The Rhetoric of Explanation: Explanatory Rhetoric from 1850 to the Present." *Written Communication* 2.1 (1985): 49–72.
—. "The Rise and Fall of the Modes of Discourse." *College Composition and Communication* 32.4 (1981): 444–55.
—. "Writing the History of Our Discipline." *An Introduction to Composition Studies*. Ed. Erika Lindemann and Gary Tate. New York: Oxford UP, 1991. 49–71.
Copeland, Charles Townsend, and H. M. Rideout. *Freshman English and Theme-Correcting in Harvard College*. New York: Silver Burdett, 1901.
Corbett, Edward P. J. *Classical Rhetoric for the Modern Student*. New York: Oxford UP, 1965.
—. "A History of Writing Program Administration." *Learning from the Histories of Rhetoric: Essays in Honor of Winifred Bryan Horner*. Ed. Theresa Enos. Carbondale, IL: Southern Illinois UP, 1993. 60–71.
—. "How I Became a Teacher of Composition." *Living Rhetoric and Composition: Stories of the Discipline*. Ed. Duane H. Roen, Stuart C. Brown, and Theresa Enos. Mahwah, NJ: Erlbaum, 1999. 1–6.
Corbett, Edward P. J., Nancy Myers, and Gary Tate, eds. *The Writing Teacher's Sourcebook*. 4th ed. New York: Oxford UP, 2000.
Council of Writing Program Administrators. "Bylaws." *WPA: Writing Program Administration* 4 (1981): 61–62.
—. "Evaluating the Intellectual Work of Writing Program Administration." *WPA: Writing Program Administration* 22.1–2 (Fall/Winter 1998): 85–104. <http://wpacouncil.org/positions/intellectualwork.html>.
Cremin, Lawrence. *American Education: The Metropolitan Experience*. New York: Harper and Row, 1988.
Crowley, Sharon. *The Methodical Memory: Invention in Current-Traditional Rhetoric*. Carbondale, IL: Southern Illinois UP, 1990.

Davis, Barbara Gross, Michael Scriven, and Susan Thomas. *The Evaluation of Composition Instruction.* Inverness, CA: Edgepress, 1981. 2nd ed. New York: Teachers College P, 1987.
Day, Henry N. *Elements of the Art of Rhetoric.* New York: W. Skinner, 1850.
Denney, Joseph V. *Two Problems in Composition Teaching.* Ann Arbor: Inland P, 1897.
Diamond, Robert M., and Bronwyn E. Adam, eds. *The Disciplines Speak: Rewarding the Scholarly, Professional, and Creative Work of Faculty.* Washington: American Association for Higher Education, 1995.
Dickson, Marcia. "Directing Without Power: Adventures in Constructing a Model for Feminist Writing Program Administration." *Writing Ourselves into the Story.* Ed. Sheryl I. Fontaine and Susan Hunger. Carbondale, IL: Southern Illinois UP, 1993. 140–53.
—. *It's Not Like That Here: Teaching Academic Writing and Reading to Novice Writers.* Portsmouth, NH: Boynton/Cook Heinemann, 1995.
Douglas, Wallace. "Barrett Wendell." *Traditions of Inquiry.* Ed. John Brereton. New York: Oxford UP, 1985. 3–25.
—. "Rhetoric for the Meritocracy: The Creation of Composition at Harvard." *English in America: A Radical View of the Profession.* Ed. Richard Ohmann. New York: Oxford UP, 1976. 97–132.
Dunn, Richard J. "Teaching Assistance, Not Teaching Assistants." *ADE Bulletin* 97 (1990): 47–50.
Elbow, Peter. *Writing without Teachers.* New York: Oxford UP, 1975.
Ebest, Sally Barr. *Changing the Way We Teach: Writing and Resistance in the Training of Teaching Assistants.* Carbondale, IL: Southern Illinois UP, 2005.
Eble, Kenneth Eugene. *The Craft of Teaching: A Guide to Mastering the Professor's Art.* 2nd ed. Jossey-Bass Series in Higher Education. San Francisco: Jossey-Bass, 1988.
Elliot, Norbert. *On a Scale: A Social History of Writing Assessment in America.* New York: Peter Lang, 2005.
Enos, Theresa. *Gender Roles and Faculty Lives in Rhetoric and Composition.* Carbondale, IL: Southern Illinois UP, 1996.
—, ed. *A Sourcebook for Basic Writing Teachers.* New York: Random House, 1987.
Ericsson, Patricia Freitag, and Richard Haswell. Machine Scoring of Student Essays: Truth and consequences. Logan, UT: Utah State UP, 2006,
"Evaluating the Intellectual Work of Writing Administration.". *Council of Writing Program Administrators.* 1998 5 December 2006 <http://wpa-council.org/positions/intellectualwork.html>.
Faculty and Administrator Modules in Higher Education (FAME). 11 November 2005. <http://telr.osu.edu/fame/index.cfm>.

Ferris, Dana. *Treatment of Error in Second Language Student Writing.* Ann Arbor, MI: U of Michigan P, 2002.

Ferris, Dana, and John S. Hedgcock. *Teaching ESL Composition: Purpose, Process, and Practice.* 2nd ed. Mahwah, NJ: Erlbaum. 2005.

Flower, Linda S., and John R. Hayes. "Problem-Solving Strategies and the Writing Process. *College English* 34.9 (1977): 449–61.

Fogerty, Daniel. *Roots for a New Rhetoric.* New York: Teachers College P, 1959.

Fulkerson, Richard. "Composition at the Turn of the Twenty-First Century." *College Composition and Communication* 56.4 (June 2005): 654–87.

Fulton, Maurice Garland. *Expository Writing.* New York: Macmillan, 1912.

Gardner, John. *On Leadership.* New York: Free P, 1990.

Gebhardt, Richard C., and Barbara Genelle Smith Gebhardt, eds. *Academic Advancement in Composition Studies: Scholarship, Publication, Promotion, Tenure.* Mahwah, NJ: Erlbaum, 1997.

George, D'Ann. "'Replacing Nice, Thin Bryn Mawr Miss Crandall with Fat, Harvard Savage': WPAs at Bryn Mawr College, 1902 to 1923." *Historical Studies of Writing Program Administration: Individuals, Communities, and the Formation of a Discipline.* Ed. Barbara L'Eplattenier and Lisa Mastrangelo. West Lafayette, IN: Parlor P, 2004. 23–36.

George, Diana, ed. *Kitchen Cooks, Plate Twirlers and Troubadours: Writing Program Administrators Tell Their Stories.* Portsmouth, NH: Boynton/Cook Heinemann, 1999.

George, Diana, and John Trimbur. "The 'Communication Battle,' or Whatever Happened to the 4th C?" *College Composition and Communication* 50 (June 1999): 682–98.

Genung, John F. *Outlines of Rhetoric: Embodied in Rules, Illustrative Examples, and a Progressive Course of Prose Composition.* Boston: Ginn, 1893.

Gerber, John C. "Loomings." 1975 ERIC Document Reproduction Service, ED 103 893.

Gibson, Walker. "Theodore Baird." *Traditions of Inquiry.* Ed. John Brereton. New York: Oxford UP, 1985. 136–52.

Glenn, Cheryl, Melissa A. Goldthwaite, and Robert Connors, eds. *The St. Martin's Guide to Teaching Writing.* 5th ed. New York: Bedford/St. Martin, 2003.

Goen, Sugie, Patricia Porter, Deborah Swanson, and Deborah Van Dommelen. "Generation 1.5." *The CATESOL Journal* 14.1 (2002): 103–69.

Goggin, Maureen Daly. *Authoring a Discipline: Scholarly Journals and the Post-World War II Emergence of Rhetoric and Composition.* Mahwah, NJ: Erlbaum, 2000.

Good, Tina LaVonne, and Leanne B. Warshauer, eds. *In Our Own Voice: Graduate Students Teach Writing.* Boston: Allyn & Bacon, 2000

Goonen, Norma M., and Rachel S. Blechman. *Higher Education Administration: A Guide to Legal, Ethical, and Practical Issues.* Westport, CT: Greenwood, 1999.

Gunner, Jeanne. "Decentering the WPA." *WPA: Writing Program Administration* 18.1–2 (Fall/Winter 1994): 8–15.

—. "Politicizing the Portland Resolution." *WPA: Writing Program Administration* 20.3 (Spring 1997): 23–30

—. "Professional Advancement of the WPA: Rhetoric and Politics in Tenure and Promotion." Ward and Carpenter, 315–30.

Hairston, Maxine. "Breaking Our Bonds and Reaffirming Our Connections." *College Composition and Communication* 36 (1985): 272-82.

—. "Winds of Change: Thomas Kuhn and the Revolution in the Teaching of Writing." *College Composition and Communication* 33 (1982): 78–86.

Hall, Anne-Marie. "Expanding the Community: A Comprehensive Look at Outreach and Articulation." *The Writing Program Administrator's Resource: A Guide to Reflective Institutional Practice.* Ed. Stuart C. Brown and Theresa Enos. Mahwah, NJ: Erlbaum, 2002. 315–30.

Halloran, S. Michael. "From Rhetoric to Composition: The Teaching of Writing in America to 1900." *A Short History of Writing Instruction: From Ancient Greece to Twentieth-Century America.* Ed. James J. Murphy. Davis, CA: Hermagoras, 1990. 151–82.

Hamp-Lyons, Liz, and William Condon. *Assessing the Portfolio: Principles for Practice, Theory, and Research.* Cresskill, NJ: Hampton Press, 2000.

Harned, Jon. "The Intellectual Background of Alexander Bain's 'Modes of Discourse.'" *College Composition and Communication* 36.1 (February 1985): 42–50.

Harper, Charles A. *A Century of Public Teacher Education: The Story of the State Teachers Colleges as They Evolved from the Normal Schools.* Westport, CT: Greenwood, 1970.

Hartwell, Patrick. "Grammar, Grammars, and the Teaching of Grammar." *College English* 47 (February 1985): 105–27.

Hartzog, Carol P. *Composition and the Academy: A Study of Writing Program Administration.* New York: MLA, 1986.

Haswell, Richard H., ed. *Beyond Outcomes: Assessment and Instruction Within a University Writing Program.* Westport, CT: Ablex, 2001.

—. "Documenting Improvement in College Writing: A Longitudinal Approach." *Written Communication* 17.3 (July 2000): 307–52.

Hawisher, Gail E., et al., eds. *Computers and the Teaching of Writing in American Higher Education, 1979–1994: A History.* Norwood, NJ: Ablex, 1996.

Heckathorn, Amy. "Moving Toward a Group Identity: WPA Professionalization from the 1940s to the 1970s." *Historical Studies of Writing Program Administration: Individuals, Communities, and the Formation of a Disci-*

pline. Ed. Barbara L'Eplattenier and Lisa Mastrangelo. West Lafayette, IN: Parlor P, 2004. 191–219.

—. "The Struggle Toward Professionalization: The Historical Evolution of Writing Program Administrators." Diss. Texas Christian U, 1999.

Herman, Arthur. *How the Scots Invented the Modern World*. New York: Three Rivers P, 2001.

Herrington, Anne, and Charles Moran. "What Happens When Machines Read Our Students' Writing?" *College English* 63.4 (March 2001): 480–99.

Hesse, Douglas D. "Politics and the WPA: Traveling Through and Past Realms of Expertise." *The Writing Program Administrator's Resource: A Guide to Reflective Institutional Practice*. Ed. Stuart C. Brown and Theresa Enos. Mahwah, NJ: Erlbaum, 2002. 41–58.

—. "Teachers as Students, Reflecting Resistance." *College Composition and Communication* 44 (1993): 224–31

—. "Understanding Larger Discourses in Higher Education: Practical Advice for WPAs." Ward and Carpenter, 299–314.

Heyda, John. "Fighting Over Freshman English: CCCC's Early Years and the Turf Wars of the 1950s." *College Composition and Communication* 50.4 (June 1999): 663–81.

—. "Industrial-Strength Composition and the Impact of Load on Teaching." *Historical Studies of Writing Program Administration: Individuals, Communities, and the Formation of a Discipline*. Ed. Barbara L'Eplattenier and Lisa Mastrangelo. West Lafayette, IN: Parlor P, 2004. 241–61.

Hilgers, Thomas L., and Joy Marsella. *Making Your Writing Program Work: A Guide to Good Practices*. Newberry Park, CA: Sage, 1992.

Hill, Adams Sherman. *The Principles of Rhetoric and Their Application*. New York: Harper, 1878.

—. *The Principles of Rhetoric*. Revised and enlarged. New York: Harper, 1895.

Hillocks, George, Jr. *Research on Written Composition: New Directions for Teaching*. Urbana, IL: NCTE, 1986.

—. *Teaching Writing as Reflective Practice*. New York: Teachers College P, 1995.

—. *The Testing Trap: How State Writing Assessments Control Learning*. New York: Teachers College P, 2002.

Holbrook, Sue Ellen. "Women's Work: The Feminizing of Composition." *Rhetoric Review* 9 (1991): 201–29.

Hopkins, Edward. *The Labor and Cost of the Teaching of English in Colleges and Secondary Schools, with Especial Reference to English Composition*. Chicago: NCTE, 1923.

Horner, Winifred Bryan. "WPA Presidents' Forum." Conference on Composition Studies in the 21st Century. Oxford, OH. Oct. 5, 2001.

Howard, Rebecca Moore. "Power Revisited: Or, How We Became a Department." *WPA: Writing Program Administration* 16.3 (1993): 37–49.
Hult, Christine A., ed. *Evaluating Teachers of Writing.* Urbana, IL: NCTE, 1994.
Hult, Christine A. "The Scholarship of Administration." *Resituating Writing: Constructing and Administering Writing Programs.* Ed. Joseph Janangelo and Kristine Hansen. Portsmouth, NH: Boynton/Cook Heinemann, 1995. 119–131.
Hult, Christine, et al. "The Portland Resolution: Council of Writing Program Administrators Guidelines for Writing Program Administrator (WPA) Positions." *WPA: Writing Program Administration* 16.1–2 (1992): 88–94.
Huot, Brian A. *(Re)articulating Writing Assessment for Teaching and Learning.* Logan: Utah State UP, 2002.
Huot, Brian A., and Ellen E. Schendel. "A Working Methodology of Assessment for Writing Program Administrators." Ward and Carpenter, 207–27.
Hunt, Lynn. "Against Presentism." President's Column, *Perspectives.* American Historical Association, May 2002. 11 November 2005. <http://www.historians.org/Perspectives/issues/2002/0205/0205pre1.cfm>
Jackson, Rebecca, and Patricia Wojahn. "Issues in Writing Program Administration: A Select Annotated Bibliography." *The Writing Program Administrator's Resource: A Guide to Reflective Institutional Practice.* Ed. Stuart C. Brown and Theresa Enos. Mahwah, NJ: Erlbaum, 2002. 467–90.
Janangelo, Joseph, and Kristine Hansen, Eds. *Resituating Writing: Constructing and Administering Writing Programs.* Crosscurrents: New Perspectives in Rhetoric and Composition. Portsmouth, NH: Boynton/Cook, 1995.
Kanter, Rosabeth Moss. *The Change Masters: Innovation and Entrepreneurship in the American Corporation.* New York: Simon and Schuster, 1983.
Kates, Susan. *Activist Rhetorics and American Higher Education, 1885–1937.* Carbondale, IL: Southern Illinois UP, 2001.
Kinkead, Joyce, and Jeanne Simpson. "The Administrative Audience: A Rhetorical Problem." Ward and Carpenter, 68–77.
Kitzhaber, Albert R. *Rhetoric in American Colleges, 1850–1900.* Dallas: Southern Methodist UP, 1990.
Klaus, Carl H., and Nancy Jones, eds. *Courses for Change in Writing: A Selection from the NEH/Iowa Institute.* Upper Montclair, NJ: Boynton/Cook, 1984.
Kroll, Barbara, ed. *Exploring the Dynamics of Second Language Writing.* Cambridge: Cambridge UP, 2003.
Kuh, George D., et al. *Student Success in College: Creating Conditions that Matter.* San Francisco: Jossey-Bass, 2005.

Laird, Charlton. "Freshman English During the Flood." *College English* 18.3 (1956): 131–38.

Latterell, Catherine G. "Training the Workforce: Overview of GTA Education Curricula." Ward and Carpenter, 139–55.

L'Epattenier, Barbara. "Finding Ourselves in the Past: An Argument for Historical Work on WPAs." *The Writing Program Administrator as Researcher.* Ed. Shirley K Rose and Irwin Weiser. Portsmouth, NH: Heinemann, 1999. 131–40.

L'Eplattenier, Barbara, and Lisa Mastrangelo, eds. *Historical Studies of Writing Program Administration: Individuals, Communities, and the Formation of a Discipline.* West Lafayette, IN: Parlor P, 2004.

Lerner, Neal. "The Teacher-Student Writing Conference and the Desire for Intimacy." *College English* 68 (2005): 186–208.

Lindblom, Kenneth and Patricia A. Dunn. "Cooperative Writing 'Program' Administration at Illinois State Normal University: The Committee on English of 1904–05 and the Influence of Professor J. Rose Colby." *Historical Studies of Writing Program Administration: Individuals, Communities, and the Formation of a Discipline.* Ed. Barbara L'Eplattenier and Lisa Mastrangelo. West Lafayette, IN: Parlor P, 2004. 37–70.

Lindemann, Erika. *A Rhetoric for Writing Teachers.* 4th ed. New York: Oxford UP, 2001.

Lloyd-Jones, Richard. "CCCC in the 1970s." E-mail to the author. 16 Jan 2005.

—. "Doing as One Likes." *Living Rhetoric and Composition: Stories of the Discipline.* Ed. Duane H. Roen, Stuart C. Brown, and Theresa Enos. Mahwah, NJ: Erlbaum, 1999. 111–121.

—. "On Institutes and Projects." *Composition in Context: Essays in Honor of Donald C. Stewart.* Ed. W. Ross Winterowd and Vincent Gillespie. Carbondale, IL: Southern Illinois UP, 1994.152–66.

—. "Who We Were, Who We Should Become." *College Composition and Communication* 43 (December 1992): 486–96.

Maid, Barry M. "Working Outside of English." Ward and Carpenter, 38–46.

Malenczyk, Rita. "Doin' the Managerial Exclusion: What WPAs Might Need to Know about Collective Bargaining." *WPA: Writing Program Administration* 27.3 (Spring 2004): 23–33.

Masters, Thomas M. *Practicing Writing: The Postwar Discourse of Freshman English.* Pittsburgh: U of Pittsburgh P, 2004.

Mastrangelo, Lisa, and Barbara L'Eplattenier. "'Is It the Pleasure of This Conference to Have Another?' Women's Colleges Meeting and Talking about Writing in the Progressive Era." L'Eplattenier and Lisa Mastrangelo, 117–43.

McKeachie, Wilbert J. and Marilla D. Svinicki. *McKeachie's Teaching Tips.* 12th ed. New York: Houghton Mifflin, 2006.

McLeod, Susan H. "The Foreigner: WAC Directors as Agents of Change." *Resituating Writing: Constructing and Administering Writing Programs.* Ed. Joseph Janangelo and Kristine Hansen. Portsmouth, NH: Boynton-Cook/Heinemann, 1995. 108–16.

—. "WAC at Century's End: Haunted by the Ghost of Fred Newton Scott." *WPA: Writing Program Administration* 21 (Fall 1997): 67–73.

Miller, Hildy. "Postmasculinist Directions in Writing Program Administration." *WPA: Writing Program Administration* 20.1.2 (1996): 49–61.

Miller, Susan. *Textual Carnivals: The Politics of Composition.* Carbondale, IL: Southern Illinois UP, 1991.

Moran, Charles. "Technology and the Teaching of Writing." *A Guide to Composition Pedagogies.* E. New York: Oxford UP, 2001. 203-23.

Murphy, James J., ed. *A Short History of Writing Instruction: From Ancient Greece to Modern America.* Davis, CA: Hermagoras, 1990.

Murray, Donald. "Teach Writing as a Process Not Product." *The Leaflet* (November 1972): 11–14. Rpt. in *Rhetoric and Composition: A Sourcebook for Teachers.* Ed. Richard Graves. New Rochelle, NJ: Hayden, 1976. 179–82.

—. *A Writer Teaches Writing.* Boston: Houghton Mifflin, 1976.

Myers-Breslin, Linda, ed. *Administrative Problem-Solving for Writing Programs and Writing Centers: Scenarios in Effective Program Management.* Urbana, IL: NCTE, 1999.

National Resource Center for the First Year Experience and Students in Transition. U of South Carolina Board of Trustees. 11 November 2005 <http://www.sc.edu/fye/>

Noonan, John P. "Two Session Workshops: 1. Administering the Large Freshman Program." *College Composition* 9 (October 1958): 174–76.

North, Stephen M. *The Making of Knowledge in Composition: Portrait of an Emerging Field.* Upper Montclair, NJ: Boynton/Cook, 1987.

Novick, Peter. *That Noble Dream: The "Objectivity Question" and the American Historical Profession.* Cambridge: Cambridge UP, 1988.

Nyquist, Jody D., ed. *Preparing the Professoriate of Tomorrow to Teach: Selected Readings in TA Training.* Dubuque, IA: Kendall/Hunt, 1991.

Nystrand, Martin, Stuart Greene, and Jeffrey Wiemelt. "Where Did Composition Studies Come From? An Intellectual History." *Written Communication* 10.3 (July 1993): 267–333.

Ohmann, Richard. *English in America: A Radical View of the Profession.* New York: Oxford UP, 1976.

—. "Professionalizing Politics." *History, Reflection, and Narrative: The Professionalization of Composition, 1963–1983.* Ed. Mary Rosner, Beth Boehm, and Debra Journet. Stamford, CT: Ablex, 1999. 227–34.

Olson, Gary A., and Joseph M. Moxley. "Directing Freshman Composition: The Limits of Authority." *College Composition and Communication* 40 (February 1989): 51–59.

Pain, Charles. *The Resistant Writer: Rhetoric as Immunity, 1850 to the Present.* Albany: SUNY UP, 1999.

Palmquist, Mike, Kate Kiefer, James Hartvigsen, and Barbara Goodlew, eds. *Transitions: Teaching Writing in Computer-Supported and Traditional Classrooms.* Greenwich, CT: Ablex, 1998.

Pantoja, Veronica, Nancy Tribbensee, and Duane Roen. "Legal Considerations for Writing Program Administrators." *The Writing Program Administrator's Resource: A Guide to Reflective Institutional Practice.* Ed. Stuart C. Brown and Theresa Enos. Mahwah, NJ: Erlbaum, 2002. 137–53.

Papp, James. "Establishment of MLA Division on the Teaching of Writing." E-mail to the author. 13 Feb 2001.

Parker, William Riley. "Where Do English Departments Come From?" *College English* 28 (1967): 339–51.

Phelps, Louise Weatherbee. *Composition as a Human Science: Contributions to the Self-Understanding of a Discipline.* New York: Oxford UP, 1988.

Popkin, Randall. "Edward Hopkins and the Costly Labor of Composition Teaching." *College Composition and Communication* 55 (June 2004): 618–41.

—. "The WPA as Publishing Scholar: Edwin Hopkins and *The Labor and Cost of Teaching English*." L'Eplattenier and Mastrangelo, 5–22.

Porter, James E. et al. "Institutional Critique: A Rhetorical Methodology for Change." *College Composition and Communication* 51 (2000): 610–41.

Purdy, Dwight. "A Polemical History of Freshman Composition in Our Time." *College English* 48 (December 1986): 791–96.

Pytlik, Betty P. "How Graduate Students Were Prepared to Teach Writing—1850–1970." Pytlik and Liggett, 3–16.

Pytlik, Betty P., and Sarah Liggett. *Preparing College Teachers of Writing: Histories, Theories, Programs, Practices.* New York: Oxford UP, 2002.

Ramey, Jack, and Pamela Takayoshi. "Watson Conference Oral History #4: Classical Rhetoric in the Present and Future of Composition Studies. October 1996, Edward P.J. Corbett, Frank D'Angelo, Winifred Horner, James Kinneavy, and C. Jan Swearingen." *History, Reflection, and Narrative: The Professionalization of Composition, 1963–1983.* Ed. Mary Rosner, Beth Boehm, and Debra Journet. Stamford, CT: Ablex, 1999. 215–23.

Reynolds, Nedra, Patricia Bizzell, and Bruce Herzberg, eds. *The Bedford Bibliography for Teachers of Writing,* 6th ed. New York: Bedford/St. Martin's, 2004. 11 November 2005. <http://www.bedfordstmartins.com/bb>.

Rhodes, Keith. "Mothers, Tell Your Children Not to Do What I have Done: The Sin and Misery of Entering the Profession as a Composition Coordinator."George, 86–94.

Robertson, Linda R., Sharon Crowley, and Frank Lentricchia, "The Wyoming Conference Resolution Opposing Unfair Salaries and Working Conditions for Post-Secondary Teachers of Writing" *College English* 49: (March 1987): 274–80.

Roen, Duane. "Writing Administration as Scholarship and Teaching." *Academic Advancement in Composition Studies: Scholarship, Publication, Promotion, Tenure.* Ed. Richard C. Gebhardt and Barbara Genelle Smith Gebhardt. Mahwah, NJ: Erlbaum, 1997. 43–55.

Roen, Duane, et al. *Strategies for Teaching First-Year Composition.* Urbana, IL: NCTE, 2002.

Rose, Shirley K., and Irwin Weiser, eds. *The Writing Program Administrator as Researcher: Inquiry in Action and Reflection.* Portsmouth, NH: Boynton/Cook Heinemann, 1999.

—. *The Writing Program Administrator as Theorist: Making Knowledge Work.* Portsmouth, NH: Boynton/Cook Heinemann, 2002.

Royer, Daniel J., and Roger Gilles, eds. *Directed Self-Placement: Principles and Practices.* Cresskill, NJ: Hampton, 2003.

Rudy, Jill Terry. "Building a Career by Directing Composition: Harvard, Professionalism, and Stith Thompson at Indiana University." L'Eplattenier and Mastrangelo, 71–88.

Russell, David R. *Writing in the Academic Disciplines, 1870–1900: A Curricular History.* 2nd ed. Carbondale, IL: Southern Illinois UP, 2002.

Ruth, Leo, and Sandra Murphy. *Designing Writing Tasks for the Assessment of Writing.* Norwood, NJ: Ablex, 1988.

Schilb, John. "The WPA and the Politics of LitComp." *The Writing Program Administrator's Resource: A Guide to Reflective Institutional Practice.* Ed. Stuart C. Brown and Theresa Enos. Mahwah, NJ: Erlbaum, 2002. 165–79.

"Scholarship in Composition: Guidelines for Faculty, Deans, and Department Chairs." *CCCC* 1987 5 December 2006 http://www.ncte.org/about/over/positions/category/write/107681.htm

Schneider, Barbara, and Richard Marback. "Judging WPAs by What they Say They Do: An Argument for Revising 'Evaluating the Intellectual Work of Writing Administration.'" *WPA: Writing Program Administration* 27.3 (Spring 2004): 7–22.

Schuster, Charles I. "The Politics of Promotion." *The Politics of Writing Instruction: Postsecondary.* Ed. Richard Bullock and John Trimbur. Portsmouth, NH: Boynton/Cook, 1991. 85–95.

Schwalm, David E. "Writing Program Administration as Preparation for an Administrative Career." *The Writing Program Administrator's Resource: A Guide to Reflective Institutional Practice.* Ed. Stuart C. Brown and Theresa Enos. Mahwah, NJ: Erlbaum, 2002.

—. "The Writing Program (Administrator) in Context: Where Am I, and Can I Still Behave Like a Faculty Member?" Ward and Carpenter, 9–22.
—. "Evaluating WPAs?" Online posting. 5 July 1994. WPA-L (Writing Program Administration Listserv). <http://lists.asu.edu/archives/wpa-l.html>.
Scott, Fred Newton, and Joseph V. Denney. *Paragraph Writing.* Boston: Allyn & Bacon, 1893.
Severino, Carol, Juan C. Guerra, and Johnella E. Butler. *Writing in Multicultural Settings.* New York: MLA, 1997.
Shamoon, Linda K., Rebecca Moore Howard, Sandra Jamieson, and Robert A. Schwegler, eds. *Coming of Age: The Advanced Writing Curriculum.* Portsmouth, NH: Boynton/Cook Heinemann, 2000.
Shaughnessy, Mina P. *Errors and Expectations: A Guide for the Teacher of Basic Writing.* New York: Oxford UP, 1977.
Shuck, Emerson C. "Administration of the Freshman English Program." *College Composition and Communication* 6 (December 1955): 205–10.
Sledd, James. "Why the Wyoming Resolution Had to Be Emasculated: A History and a Quixotism." *JAC* 11.2 (1991): 269–81.
Smit, David. "Curriculum Design for First-Year Writing Programs." Ward and Carpenter, 185–206.
Smith, William L. "Assessing the Reliability of Using Holistic Scoring of Essays as a College Composition Placement Technique." Williamson and Huot, 142–205.
Solomon, Barbara Miller. *In the Company of Educated Women.* New Haven: Yale UP, 1985.
Spring, Joel. *The American School, 1642–1985.* New York: Longman, 1986.
"Statement on Class Size and Workload: College." *NCTE* 1987. 5 December 2006 <http://www.ncte.org/about/over/positions/category/class/107626.htm>.
"Statement from the Conference on the Growing Use of Part-Time and Adjunct Faculty." *NCTE* 1997 5 December 2006 <http://www.ncte.org/about/over/positions/category/profcon/107662.htm>.
"Statement on Non-Tenure-Track Faculty Members." *MLA.* 2003. 5 December 2006. <http://www.mla.org/statement_on_nonten>.
Stewart, Donald C. "Harvard's Influence on English Studies." *College Composition and Communication* 43 (December 1992): 455–71.
—. "A Model for Our Time: Fred Newton Scott's Rhetoric Program at Michigan." *Learning from the Histories of Rhetoric: Essays in Honor of Winifred Bryan Horner.* Ed. Theresa Enos. Carbondale, IL: Southern Illinois UP, 1993. 42–59.
—. "Rediscovering Fred Newton Scott." *College English* 40 (1979): 539–47.

—. "Two Model Teachers and the Harvardization of English Departments." *The Rhetorical Tradition and Modern Writing.* Ed. James J. Murphy. New York: MLA, 1982. 118–29.

Stewart, Donald C., and Patricia Stewart. *The Life and Legacy of Fred Newton Scott.* Pittsburgh: U of Pittsburgh P, 1997.

Strenski, Ellen. "Helping TAs across the Curriculum Teach Writing: An Additional Use for the TA Handbook." *WPA: Writing Program Administration* 15.3 (1992): 68–73.

Strickland, Donna. "Taking Dictation: The Emergence of Writing Programs and the Cultural Contradictions of Composition Teaching." *College English* 63 (2001): 457–79.

Tate, Gary, Amy Rupiper, and Kurt Schick, eds. *A Guide to Composition Pedagogies.* New York: Oxford UP, 2001.

Taylor, Todd. "Ten Commandments for Computers and Composition." Ward and Carpenter, 228–42.

Tobin, Lad. "How the Writing Process Movement Was Born—And Other Conversion Narratives." *Taking Stock: The Writing Process Movement in the 90s.* Ed. Lad Tobin and Thomas Newkirk. Portsmouth, NH: Boynton/Cook-Heinemann, 1994. 1–14.

Trachsel, Mary. *Institutionalizing Literacy: The Historical Role of College Entrance Examinations in English.* Carbondale, IL: Southern Illinois UP, 1992.

Varnum, Robin. *Fencing with Words: A History of Writing Instruction at Amherst College during the Era of Theodore Baird, 1938–1966.* Urbana, IL: NCTE, 1996.

Veysey, Laurence. R. *The Emergence of the American University.* Chicago: U of Chicago P, 1965.

Ward, Irene. "Developing Healthy Management and Leadership Styles: Surviving the WPA's 'Inside Game.'" Ward and Carpenter, 49–67.

Ward, Irene, and William J. Carpenter, eds. *The Allyn & Bacon Sourcebook for Writing Program Administrators.* New York: Allyn & Bacon, 2002.

Ward, Irene, and Merry Perry. "A Selection of Strategies for Training Teaching Assistants." Ward and Carpenter, 117–38.

Weaver, Constance. *Teaching Grammar in Context.* Portsmouth, NH: Boynton/Cook, 1996.

Wendell, Barrett. *English Composition: Eight Lectures Given at the Lowell Institute.* New York: Scribners, 1891.

White, Edward M. *Assigning, Responding, Evaluating: A Writing Teacher's Guide.* 4th ed. New York: Bedford, Freeman, Worth, 2007.

—. *Developing Successful College Writing Programs.* San Francisco: Jossey-Bass, 1989.

—. "The Scoring of Writing Portfolios: Phase 2." *College Composition and Communication* 56.4 (June 2005): 581–600.

—. *Teaching and Assessing Writing.* 2nd ed. San Francisco: Jossey-Bass, 1994.
—. "Use It or Lose It: Power and the WPA." *WPA: Writing Program Administration* 15.1–2 (1991): 3–12.
Wiener, Harvey. "Early History of WPA." E-mails to the author. 25 November 2000, 4 April 2005.
—. Personal interview. 16 March 2001.
Wilhoit, Stephen. "Recent Trends in TA Instruction: A Bibliographic Essay." Pytlik and Liggett, 17–27.
Williamson, Michael M., and Brian A. Huot. *Validating Holistic Scoring for Writing Assessment: Theoretical and Empirical Foundations.* Cresskill, NJ: Hampton, 1993.
Witte, Stephen P., and Lester Faigley. *Evaluating College Writing Programs.* Carbondale, IL: Southern Illinois UP, 1983.
Wolcott, Willa, and Sue M. Legg, *An Overview of Writing Assessment: Theory, Research, and Practice.* Urbana, IL: NCTE, 1998.
Woods, William F. "Nineteenth-Century Psychology and the Teaching of Writing." *College Composition and Communication* 36.1 (February 1985): 20–41.
Wozniak, John Michael. *English Composition in Eastern Colleges, 1850–1940.* Washington, D.C.: UP of America, 1978.
Yale Report. 1828. 2 December 2006. <http://www.higher-ed.org/resources/Yale_Report.htm>.
Yancey, Kathleen Blake. "Looking Back as We Look Forward: Historicizing Writing Assessment." *College Composition and Communication* 50 (1999): 483–503.
Yancey, Kathleen Blake, et al. "The Portraits of Composition Study of Writing: Design Features and Some Preliminary Findings." Conference on Writing Research in the Making. Santa Barbara, CA, Feb. 5–6, 2005.
Yancey, Kathleen Blake, and Irwin Weiser, eds. *Situating Portfolios: Four Perspectives.* Logan, UT: Utah State UP, 1997.
Young, Richard. "Paradigms and Problems: Needed Research in Rhetorical Invention." *Research on Composing: Points of Departure.* Ed. Charles R. Cooper and Lee Odell. Urbana, IL: NCTE, 1978. 29–48.
Zelnick, Stephen. "A Report on the Workshop on the Administration of Writing Programs, Summer, 1982." *WPA: Writing Program Administration* 6 (Spring 1983): 11–14.

Index

academic affairs, 10, 20. *See also* higher education administration
academic discourse, 82–83, 91
accountability, 4, 14–15, 73, 81, 92–97, 101, 106, 120–123. *See also* higher education administration
accreditation, 106, 109, 112
ADE Bulletin, 106, 117
administrative discourse, 101. *See also* higher education administration
advanced composition, 10, 81, 88–89
advanced placement exam, 93, 106, 108. *See also* standardized tests
affirmative action, 69, 98, 111–112, 132n
American Association of Colleges and Universities, 105, 112
American Association of Community Colleges, 69
American Association of Journalism Teachers, 47
American Association of University Professors (AAUP), 105
American Revolution, 25
American universities, 25, 28; history of, 23–26, 28, 31, 39, 40–46, 48, 51 , 53 , 56 , 58–59, 61, 67, 72–73 , 82
Americans with Disabilities Act, 106

Amherst College, 39, 46, 62, 134n
Amorose, Thomas, 8
Annales School, 24
Anson, Chris M., 101, 115
Anti-War Movement, 68
argumentation, 38–39, 42, 81–82, 133n
articulation, 8, 14, 88, 106. *See also* secondary schools
assessment, 4, 9–10,14, 16–17, 28, 72–73, 75, 81, 87, 92–97, 120–123, 126; Dynamic Criteria Mapping, 121; institutional, 14, 16, 72, 92–93, 96–97, 112, 123; portfolios, 90, 92–97, 100, 121–123; proficiency, 66, 92, 96, 134n; program, 14, 16, 72, 92–93, 96–97, 112, 123; reliability, 93, 95, 123; validity, 93, 121, 123
Association of American Colleges, 78, 101
Association of Departments of English (ADE), 26, 80, 92, 98, 106, 117
Astin, Helen, 21
Atwan, Bob, 134n
Aydelotte, Frank, 37

Bain, Alexander, 39–41
Baird, Theodore, 62–63, 134n
Barnard College, 51
Bartholomae, David, 63, 86, 134n
Baruch College, 70

153

basic writing, 10, 60, 66, 69–70, 81, 85–87, 91, 95, 98, 114, 119–120, 129
Bay Area Writing Project, 96
Bazerman, Charles, 70
Belanoff, Pat, 90, 96
Belcher, Diane, 87
belles lettres, 37
Berlin, James, 29, 41, 46–47, 56–57
Birnbaum, Robert, 101
Bishop, Wendy, 73–75
Bizzell, Patricia, 73, 82, 114, 134n
Blechman, Rachel S., 101, 129
Bloom, Lynn Z., 12, 72, 78, 129
Bordelon, Suzanne, 49, 53–54
Born, Margaret, 101
Boston University, 20
Bousquet, Marc, 19
Boyer, Ernest, 15, 77, 104, 128
Boylston Professor of Rhetoric, 29, 48, 132n
Braddock, Richard, 62, 68
Bradley University, 56
Brereton, John, 29–30, 32–33, 35, 37, 46, 49, 52, 60, 70, 133n, 134n
Briggs, LeBaron Russell, 32–35
Britton, James, 82
Broad, Bob, 120–121
Brooklyn College, 70
Brookwood Labor College, 37
Brown, Rollo, 32–35
Brown, Stuart, 80, 102, 115, 132n
Bruffee, Kenneth, 17, 70–71, 77–78
Bryn Mawr, 5, 51, 54
Buck, Gertrude, 37, 47, 52–54, 133n
Buckley Amendment, 80, 109
budget, 4, 8, 10, 74, 76, 98, 101, 108, 110–113, 127, 133n
Bullock, Richard, 73, 75

Burnham, Christopher, 91, 120
Bushman, Donald, 16

Cambridge, Barbara L., 21, 96
Campbell, JoAnn, 51–52, 54, 133n
Carnegie classification, 107
Carnegie Corporation, 96
Carnegie Foundation, 107
Carnegie Mellon, 89
Carnegie unit, 108
Carpenter, William, 80
Catalano, Timothy, 100
CATESOL Journal, 88
CCCC, 60, 62–67, 69, 71–72, 74, 78, 80, 86, 91, 94, 98, 108, 118, 134n
Cheramie, Deany M., 55
Chief Academic Officer, 10, 108
Child, Francis, 48
City College, 70
Civil Rights Movement, 68, 109, 134n
Civil War, 25, 28, 44, 55, 58
class size, 9, 50, 55, 66, 80, 91–92, 98, 109, 117
Clemson University, 82
CLEP, 93, 108. *See also* standardized tests
Colby, J. Rose, 51
collaboration, 13, 17, 47, 53, 88, 90, 91, 120, 126
College Board, 94, 106, 108. *See also* standardized tests
College Composition and Communication, 65–66, 78
College English, 37, 117
College Entrance Examination Board, 68, 108
College of William and Mary, 132n
Columbia University, 38

committee structure, 108. *See also* higher education administration
common school movement, 132n
communication studies, 65
community colleges, 69, 106
Composition Studies, 77, 89
computers and composition, 91, 118, 119, 120, 131
Computers and Composition (journal), 91
Condon, William, 121
Conference of Writing Program Administrators, 18, 75
Conference on Basic Writing, 86
conference workshops, 63–65, 68, 71–72, 75, 78
Connors, Robert, 23, 24, 25–26, 31, 32, 39, 41–42, 48, 59
contact hours, 109
Copeland, C. T., 34, 36
Corbett, Edward P.J., 30–31, 58, 61, 63–64, 70, 100, 118, 133n
Cornell University, 57, 71, 133n
Council of Writing Program Administrators, 3, 11, 14, 59, 64, 67–78, 80, 85, 97, 103, 112, 115, 128, 132n; Consultant-Evaluator Program, 72, 80, 97, 112, 115; Executive Committee, 71; funding of, 72
Covino, William A., 120, 135n
Crandall, Regina, 54–55
critical pedagogy, 83, 91. *See also* cultural studies
Crossley, Gay Lynn, 74
Crowley, Sharon, 39
cultural studies, 82–83, 91, 120
CUNY, 69–71, 86
current-traditional rhetoric, 5, 24, 27–28, 38–39, 42, 47, 52, 60, 67, 82, 90, 133n
curriculum, 4, 9, 16, 25–28, 30–31, 35, 37–38, 41, 43–44, 47, 51, 54–55, 59, 62, 73, 81–89, 96–97, 99, 102, 117–120, 133n, 135n. *See also* first-year composition

D'Angelo, Frank, 133n
Daiker, Donald A., 78
Dartmouth College, 132n
Davis, Barbara, 96
Day, Henry, 41
Denney, Joseph V., 42, 45, 47
development office, 107, 109. *See also* higher education administration
Dewey, John, 16, 53, 105
Dickson, Marcia, 13, 86, 96
disciplinarity, 15–16, 23–24, 27–28, 32–33, 39, 42–43, 48, 57, 59, 65, 67–68, 73, 86, 89, 117
doctoral programs, 68, 73, 74
Donovan, Tim, 71
Douglas, Wallace, 33, 132n
Dunn, Patricia, 50
Dunn, Richard J., 124

Ebest, Sally Barr, 124, 132n
Eble, Kenneth Eugene, 124–125
Educational Opportunity Program, 109
Elbow, Peter, 89–90, 96
Eliot, Charles W., 28,-29, 31, 33
English Composition Card, 34
English departments, 3, 5, 8, 12, 18, 24–32, 37–38, 42, 44, 48–54, 56, 58, 62–63, 68–69, 72–73, 75, 81, 98, 100–104, 106, 111–112, 128–129, 133–135n
Enos, Theresa, 12, 80, 85, 115, 129

enrollment, 25–27, 45, 49, 56, 58, 61, 64–65, 67–69, 98, 111, 112, 133n
Ericsson, Patricia Freitag, 94
error, 9, 26, 29, 43–44, 52, 56, 60, 85–88, 118, 125, 133n
ethnography, 83, 86
Exxon Foundation, 72

Faculty and Administrator Modules in Higher Education (FAME), 86
faculty unions, 19–20, 100
Faigley, Lester, 96–97
FERPA, 102, 109
Ferris, Dana, 87, 118
FIPSE, 110
first-year composition, 5, 26, 28–29, 33, 45, 51, 56, 73, 81, 83, 85, 88, 91, 93, 95, 98, 106, 125
Flower, Linda, 89, 134n
Fogerty, Daniel, 38
Fulkerson, Richard, 82, 135n
full-time equivalent, 101, 110. *See also* administrative discourse
Fulton, Maurice Garland, 42
fund-raising, 107–110. *See also* development office

G.I. Bill, 45, 58
Gage, John, 28
Gardner, John, 21
Gebhardt, Barbara, 103, 129
Gebhardt, Richard, 72, 103, 129
general education, 44, 81, 106, 108, 110
genre, 82, 86
Genung, John Franklin, 39, 46
George, Ann, 91, 120
George, D'Ann, 54
George, Diana, 65, 73–74, 91, 120
Gerber, John, 63–64, 66

German university model, 24–26, 29, 31, 48
Gibson, Walker, 62, 134n
Glenn, Cheryl, 99
goals statement, 96, 110. *See also* higher education administration
Goggin, Maureen, 68
Goonen, Norma M., 101, 129
graduate students, 3, 7–9, 12, 18–19, 31–32, 47, 57, 61, 67, 69, 81, 99–100, 102, 110, 118, 122, 124–126, 127, 130, 135n
Gunner, Jeanne, 9, 103, 134n

Halloran, S. Michael, 133n
Hamp-Lyons, Liz, 121
Harned, Jon, 40–41
Hart, Albert Bushnell, 48
Hartwell, Patrick, 86
Hartzog, Carol, 68
Harvard University, 11, 24, 28–35, 37, 46–48, 50–52, 54, 55–57, 92, 132n, 133n
Haswell, Richard, 94–95, 97
Hayes, John, 89
Heckathorn, Amy, 17, 59, 68
Hedgecock, John, 118
Herrington, Anne, 94
Herzberg, Bruce, 82, 114, 134n
Hesse, Douglas D., 17, 101–102, 115, 125, 129
Heyda, John, 45, 65
higher education administration, 9, 11, 19, 79, 97, 100–101, 127, 130
Hilgers, Thomas, 80, 83–84, 98–99
Hill, Adams Sherman, 29–30, 32–35, 46, 48, 132n, 133n
Hillocks, George, 90, 93, 118–119
Hirvela, Alan, 87
historically Black colleges (HBCUs), 55, 110

Index 157

Hobson, Eric H., 120, 135n
Holbrook, Sue Ellen, 12
holistic scoring, 92–96, 113, 123
Hopkins, Edward, 45, 49, 50
Horner, Winifred Bryan, 70, 133n
Hostos Community College, 70
Howard, Rebecca Moore, 13, 55, 91, 120
Hult, Christine, 15, 75, 77, 99, 125, 129
human resources, 110
Huot, Brian A., 93–94, 121

IDEA, 110
Illinois State Normal University, 51
in loco parentis, 43
Indiana University, 37, 57, 111
indirect costs, 110. *See also* budget
Institutional Review Board, 111
Intercollege Conference on English Composition, 63

JAC: A Journal of Composition Theory, 89
Jarratt, Susan C., 91, 120
Johns Hopkins University, 48
Jones, Nancy, 61, 68
Jossey-Bass, 100–101
Julier, Laura, 91, 120

Kairos, 91
Kanter, Rosabeth Moss, 5
Kates, Susan, 37
Kinkead, Joyce, 101, 130
Kinneavy, James, 82, 133n
Kitzhaber, Albert, 28, 39, 46–48
Klaus, Carl, 68
Kroll, Barbara, 87, 129

L'Eplattenier, Barbara, 45, 63
Laird, Charlton, 65
land grant universities, 25
Legg, Sue M., 93, 123

Leland, Carol, 21
liberal arts education, 7, 27, 41, 44, 71, 81, 105
Liberal Education (journal), 105
Lindbloom, Kenneth, 50
Lindemann, Erika, 100
line items, 111. *See also* budget
line positions, 10. *See also* tenure
Linguistic Society of America, 26
Lloyd-Jones, Richard, 61–63, 68, 134n
Lounsbury, Thomas, 37
Lyons, Bob, 70

Maid, Barry, 102
Maimon, Elaine, 70, 78
Malenczyk, Rita, 19
Marsella, Joy, 80, 83, 98–99
Masters, Thomas, 24, 59–60
Mastrangelo, Lisa, 49, 63
McAllister, Ken S., 115
McClelland, Ben W., 21
McCosh, James, 44
McKeachie, Wilbert J., 126
McLeod, Susan, 17, 115, 120, 129, 133n, 135n
McQuade, Don, 70, 134n
Mead, George Herbert, 16
Middle States Association of Colleges and Schools, 72, 97
Miller, Hildy, 13
Miller, Susan, 133n
mission statements, 110, 110. *See also higher education administration*
MLA, 26, 46, 59, 63, 68, 70–71, 78, 92, 106, 111, 127, 130, 133n; *Job Information List,* 59, 68
Moffett, James, 82
Moran, Charles, 91, 94, 120
Morill Act, 25
Mount Holyoke College, 49, 63

Moxley, Joseph, 74
Murphy, James J., 23
Murphy, Sandra, 94
Murray, Donald, 67, 89
Mutnick, Deborah, 91, 120
Myers-Breslin, Linda, 80, 130

NASULGC, 111
National Defense Education Act, 68
National Education Association (NEA), 27
National Labor Relations Act of 1935 (NLRA), 19–20
National Labor Relations Board (NLRB), 19
National Resource Center for the First Year Experience and Students in Transition, 81
National Survey of Student Engagement (NSSE), 111
National Writing Project (NWP), 68, 88
NCTE, 9, 46, 50, 61, 63, 69, 78, 80, 91, 98, 108, 111, 117–118, 123, 125, 127–128, 130
New York Magazine, 132n
Noonan, John P., 73
Normal Schools, 25
North Carolina State University, 57
North, Stephen, 46, 57, 73, 133n
Northeastern University, 71
Northwestern University, 59
Nystrand, Martin, 83

Ohmann, Richard, 70, 76
Olson, Gary, 74
Ombuds, 112

Pain, Charles, 45
Pantoja, Veronica, 101
Parker, William Riley, 26, 102

pedagogy, 4, 6–11, 13–14, 17–18, 21–22, 24, 26, 28–30, 32–44, 46–47, 49–50, 52–55, 60–68, 73, 76, 81–86, 88–93, 96–100, 103–104, 107, 110–111, 116–128, 133n, 134n, 135n; assignments, 24, 35, 52, 62, 84, 90, 118, 122, 134n; expressivism, 91; modes, 39, 40, 41, 44, 90, 125, 128; process, 38, 66–67, 72, 82–85, 87, 89–91, 95–96, 119–120; response to student writing, 8, 9, 34, 55, 56, 63, 70, 75, 78, 84, 87, 107, 121–122, 125, 126
peer institutions, 109
Peer Review (journal), 105
peer review, 90, 126, 127
peer tutoring, 65
Perl, Sondra, 70
Petrosky, Anthony, 86
Phelps, Louise Weatherbee, 16
placement, 8–10, 30, 56–57, 66, 73, 92–97, 122, 123; directed self-placement, 9, 95, 122plagiarism, 8, 87, 102. *See also* assessment
Popkin, Randall, 45, 50
Porter, James, 19
Portland Resolution, 14, 75, 77, 80, 112, 129, 132n, 134n
Princeton University, 25, 35, 44, 128, 132n
Progressive Era, 53, 63
Purdue University, 3, 57, 66
Purdy, Dwight, 67, 73
Pytlik, Betty, 57, 100

Queens College, 70

Radcliffe College, 51
reading, 5, 12, 23, 28, 44, 61–62, 64–65, 82, 87, 95–96, 118, 125

Index

Responsibility Centered Budget/Management, 112. *See also* budget
rhetorical education, 4, 5, 8, 19, 23, 26–32, 37–38, 40, 42, 44, 46–53, 68, 73, 77, 82, 98, 103, 133n
Rhodes, Keith, 74
Rideout, H. M., 34, 36
Roberts, Charles Walter, 60
Roen, Duane, 99, 103, 129
Rose, Shirley, 16, 116
Royer, Daniel, 95, 122
Rudy, Jill Terry, 57
Rush, Benjamin, 43
Russell, David, 30, 65, 69
Rutgers University, 132n, 134n
Ruth, Leo, 94

SAT, 9, 108, 112. *See also* standardized tests
Savage, Howard, 54, 55
Schell, Eileen E., 115
Schendel, Ellen E., 93
Schuster, Charles, 12, 103
Schwalm, David, 8, 10, 21, 45, 78
Scott, Fred Newton, 37, 42, 46–52, 133n
secondary schools, 60
Selfe, Cynthia L., 115
service learning, 8, 83
Shamoon, Linda K., 89
shared governance, 113. *See also* higher education administration
Shaughnessy, Mina, 69, 70, 85
Shuck, Emerson, 66
Silva, Tony, 87
Simpson, Jeanne, 101, 130
Sisters of the Blessed Sacrament, 56
Sledd, James, 18, 55, 75
Smit, David, 82
Smith College, 37, 51, 63
Smith, William, 94–95

social constructionism, 47, 96
soft money, 113. *See also* budget
Speech Association of America, 26
Spring, Joel, 43, 132n
standardized tests, 9, 94, 108, 112
Stewart, Donald, 46–49, 133n
Stewart, Patricia, 46–47, 49
strategic plan, 113
Strenski, Ellen, 127
Strickland, Donna, 18
student credit hours, 101, 113
students; African American, 25, 37, 55, 69, 94; Asian American, 94; diverse backgrounds of, 69; ESL, 87–88, 109, 118; generation 1.5, 87–88, 109; veterans, 58, 61, 64–65, 68; women, 25, 37, 51–52, 54
Stygall, Gail, 115
Supreme Court, 19, 132n
Swearingen, C. Jan, 133n
Syfer, Judy, 12
Syracuse University, 56

Taylor, Todd, 91
temporary dollars, 113. *See also* budget
tenure, 4, 8, 11–12, 14, 32, 67, 73–74, 76–77, 101, 103, 105, 108, 112–113, 127–129, 132n
textbooks, 28–29, 33, 37–42, 44, 46–47, 52, 57, 82–84, 99, 135n
The Journal of Basic Writing, 86
The Ohio State University, 86
Thomas, M. Carey, 54–55
Thompson, Stith, 57
Tobin, Lad, 89–90, 120
Trachsel, Mary, 29
Trimbur, John, 65, 91, 120
Two-Year College English Association, 69

UCLA, 57
University of Alaska, Anchorage, 78
University of Illinois, 51, 57, 59, 60, 124
University of Iowa, 61, 133n
University of Kansas, 49, 50, 133n
University of Michigan, 37, 46–53, 132–133n
University of Minnesota, 57
University of Pittsburgh, 94
University of Vermont, 20
University of West Virginia, 57
University of Wisconsin, 38, 57, 133n
unrestricted funds, 113. *See also* budget

Varnum, Robin, 62–63, 134n
Vassar College, 49, 51–53, 55, 63, 133n
Veysey, Laurence, 25, 44

Ward, Irene, 20, 80, 100, 104, 116
Washington State University, 3, 95, 97
Weaver, Constance, 87
Weiser, Irwin, 16, 96, 116, 123
Wellesley College, 49, 51, 63
Wendell, Barrett, 33, 35, 37, 46
Wheaton College, 60
White, Edward M., 13, 75, 78, 80–81, 92–94, 96–97, 99, 115, 122
Wiener, Harvey, 70–72, 97
Wilhoit, Stephen, 100
Williamson, Michael, 94
Witherspoon, John, 25
Witte, Stephen, 96–97
Wolcott, Willa, 93, 123
Woods, William, 40, 43
World War I, 46

World War II, 45, 58–59, 61, 63, 68, 72
Wozniak, John Michael, 30
WPA Listserv, 78, 99, 117
WPA Outcomes Statement, 44, 80, 85, 103
WPA: A Newsletter for Writing Program Administration, 71
WPA: Writing Program Administration, 14, 71–72, 75, 78, 100, 115, 117
writing across the curriculum, 7, 10, 15, 17, 51, 99, 120, 126–127, 131, 133n
writing instructors; adjunct faculty, 7–8, 115, 99, 126–127; development of, 4, 9, 14, 16, 67, 81, 96, 98–100, 117, 123–128, 131; evaluation of, 4, 8, 84, 98–100, 102, 125–126, 128; hiring of, 4, 8, 58, 61, 73, 81, 98–100, 102–103, 124–130; salaries of, 12, 51, 53–55, 99; supervision of, 3, 7, 19, 70, 104, 127; teaching assistants as, 8, 12, 18–19, 68–69, 99–100, 122, 124–127; training of, 4, 8–9, 12, 14, 16, 27, 55, 57, 61, 67, 69, 73–74, 81, 91, 96, 98–100, 102, 104, 117, 123–128, 130, 131, 135n; treatment of, 32
writing portfolios, 90, 92–94, 96–97, 121–123
writing program administration; as intellectual work, 3, 7, 11, 14–16, 21, 75–77, 80, 82, 103, 128; as service, 3, 8, 11–12, 15–16, 22, 73–74, 104, 116, 128, 130; nature of, 4, 8–9, 11, 28, 35, 50, 67, 71, 101, 115–116, 128–130; politics of, 12, 23, 83, 101–103, 115–116; role of context in, 7–8, 22, 24, 38, 46, 49, 54, 79,

83–84, 93, 96, 101–102, 105, 115–116, 123, 135n
writing program administrators; advancement of, 57–58; constraints put upon, 23, 29, 55, 61, 74–75, 93, 96, 98, 104; definitions of, 5, 20, 72, 75; identity of, 7–23; institutional position of, 9; job descriptions of, 104; professionalization of, 58, 77; salaries of, 53, 55; women as, 11–14, 52–55 work load of, 53, 67

Wylie, Laura Johnson, 53
Wyoming Resolution, 134n

Xavier University, 55

Yale Report of 1828, 43, 44
Yale University, 37, 43, 44, 66
Yancey, Kathleen Blake, 82, 92, 96, 98, 123
Yeshiva University, 19
Young, Richard, 28, 38–39

Zelnick, Stephen, 71

www.ingramcontent.com/pod-product-compliance
Lightning Source LLC
Chambersburg PA
CBHW030139240426
43672CB00005B/196